THIS IS THE YEAR

The historic 2008 Chicago Cubs

Chicago Tribune

This book is available
in quantity at special
discounts for your group
or organization. For
further information,
contact:
Triumph Books, 542 S.
Dearborn Street, Suite 750
Chicago, IL 60605,
Phone: (312) 939-3330,
Fax: (312) 663-3557
Printed in U.S.A.

ISBN: 978-1-60078-242-8

Front and back cover
photos by
PHIL VELASQUEZ

Jack Brickhouse
1916–1998

This book is dedicated to
Jack Brickhouse, the inimitable
and cheerful "Voice of the Cubs"
for more than three decades. His
broadcasts brought the joy of
baseball to two generations of
Chicago sports fans, helping
them become the world's best.
And his relentless optimism in
the face of nearly constant
disappointment personified what
it meant to be a Cubs fan.

The 100-year anniversary

JACK BRICKHOUSE, the Cubs' irrepressibly sunny broadcast voice for more than three decades, was kidding when he summed up the team's inglorious history of underachievement with a classic observation:

"Any team can have a bad century."

He was kidding ... wasn't he?

Brickhouse made that statement back in the 1970s, as the nucleus of the ill-fated 1969 near-missers was being scattered to the wind and the Cubs were starting over again. Little did he know the championship drought he had witnessed would extend another 30-plus years and indeed reach the brink of the century mark.

Thus the urgency attached to the 2008 season. It marks an even 100 years since the team's last World Series title.

The White Sox and their fans saw their dream come true in 2005, after a "mere" 88 years. It gave their city a giddy sense that anything is possible. But a Cubs fan's skepticism is understandable — a century of deprivation will do that to even the truest believer.

The Cubs have long since shed their "lovable losers" image. And they're in the playoffs for the fourth time in 11 seasons, their best stretch of baseball since the 1930s. But they have advanced beyond the first round only once in that span. And that trip to the cusp of the World Series in 2003 ended in infamous heartbreak ... as it so often does for the Cubs and their long-suffering fans.

Thus the urgency attached to the 2008 season. It was going to be different. Lou Piniella had a year's familiarity to call on in shaping the team to his liking. Pitching, fielding, power, speed ... there were no noticeable shortcomings. And general manager Jim Hendry made moves to deepen a roster that had improved markedly over the course of 2007, only to endure a first-round playoff flameout that overshadowed many of the good things that had happened.

Once again there was hope, the lifeblood of the true Cubs fan.

Could this be The Year?

Previous page
Jack Brickhouse saw plenty of long seasons at Wrigley Field, but he never lost his sunny attitude.
CHRIS WALKER

CONTENTS

FOREWORDS
Ron Santo **18**
Ernie Banks **20**

COLUMNISTS
Rick Morrissey **22**
Mike Downey **23**
Phil Rogers **24**
Paul Sullivan **25**

CHAPTER 1
Getting ready **40**

CHAPTER 2
The first half **44**

CHAPTER 3
The City Series **52**

CHAPTER 4
The All-Star Cubs **56**

CHAPTER 5
Four days in Milwaukee **62**

CHAPTER 6
The stretch drive **66**

PHOTO ESSAY
By Chris Walker **114**

**BASEBALL CARDS
AND STATS 121**

OUT LOUDS
Kerry Wood **76**
Ted Lilly **82**
Jeff Samardzija **86**
Jason Marquis **90**
Aramis Ramirez **102**

PROFILES
Lou Piniella **28**
Jim Hendry **34**
Ryan Dempster **78**
Carlos Zambrano **84**
Carlos Marmol **88**
Derrek Lee **94**

Mark DeRosa **96**
Ryan Theriot/Mike Fontenot **98**
Alfonso Soriano **106**
Jim Edmonds **108**
Reed Johnson **110**
Kosuke Fukudome **112**

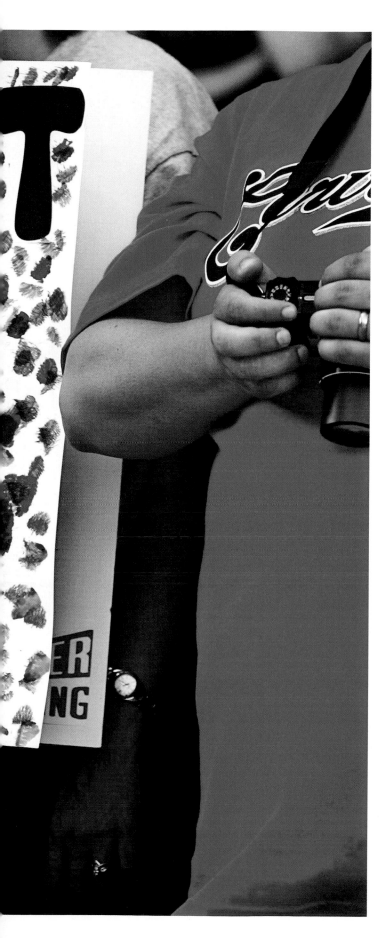

Previous pages
2-3 The stadium marquee says it all: Wrigley was indeed the Friendly Confines for a Cubs team that was dominant at home.
PHIL VELASQUEZ

6-7 The eerie double rainbow June 22 at Wrigley Field was prophetic: The Cubs swept the White Sox.
SCOTT STRAZZANTE

8-9 As the ivy on the outfield walls brightened, so did the Cubs' fortunes in this championship season.
PHIL VELASQUEZ

10-11 Like a jockey on a thoroughbred, Mike Fontenot gets a ride on the back of Carlos Zambrano, who was a horse in beating the Brewers on July 29.
NUCCIO DINUZZO

12-13 Each baseball has 108 stitches, and each game seemed to bring that many thrills to Cubs fans.
PHIL VELASQUEZ

The Cubs added new fans like Addison Kobler during their championship season. **NUCCIO DINUZZO**

A young fan enjoys his Derrek Lee bobblehead.
PHIL VELASQUEZ

Some fans were brave in trying to catch this home run ball; other fans, not so much. **PHIL VELASQUEZ**

RON SANTO

THE CHICAGO CUBS FRATERNITY extends back many, many decades, and I am proud to feel a connection with the dynamic 2008 edition that captured the division championship while capturing the hearts of our loyal fans.

We were a very entertaining ballclub in 1969. We had three Hall of Famers — Ernie Banks, Billy Williams and Fergie Jenkins — and we related well to the fans. We posed for pictures, and we knew that when we walked down by the left-field line at Wrigley Field, we would all sign autographs. We said hi to everybody. It was a wonderful love affair. The fans made us feel like rock stars.

As a Cubs broadcaster for WGN radio now, I have seen that same environment engulf Wrigley Field 39 years later. I regret that we were unable to deliver a World Series championship to our fans back in '69. They deserved it.

Back in those days, the players' families were close, and not that many guys from the nucleus of our team got traded. When we did get traded, it was at the end of our careers. We remain close to this day.

Being a Cub is a lifetime designation. People often ask me about my desire to one day be voted into the Hall of Fame. No doubt, that would be a huge accomplishment. But my Hall of Fame feeling already came when the Cubs honored me by retiring my number on Sept. 28, 2003.

I played in 1,012 Cubs victories during my career of 14 years with the Cubs. Seeing the Cubs win a World Series is my lifelong dream.

Ron Santo took us out to the ballgame for 14 glorious years as a player. **PHIL VELASQUEZ**

ERNIE BANKS

WHAT A MEMORABLE YEAR this has been for both me and the Chicago Cubs.

First, the Cubs honored me with a statue in front of Wrigley Field. They made me feel immortal! The statue will be here long after I am spreading cheer and encouraging teams by saying, "Let's Play Two!"

The Cubs' marvelous 2008 season was the icing on the cake for me and this franchise's faithful legion of fans. Winning the division and advancing to the playoffs answered a lot of folks' prayers. I wish I could have played for the 2008 Cubs.

I still take great pride in being known as "Mr. Cub."

That's kind of what my life has always been about. I wanted to finish my career with one team, in one city, one mayor, one park, one owner. I did that. When I first started, Mayor Richard J. Daley was the mayor. The Wrigleys owned the team. We played all of our home games at Wrigley Field during the daytime. So my career was very unique, and I am proud of it.

I have been involved in the city of Chicago and with Little Leagues all around the city and suburbs. It was a fun and enjoyable time. Now I meet a lot of people who used to come out to Wrigley Field when they were kids, and they are in their 50s now. They still remember those days.

This book not only celebrates the 2008 Cubs of manager Lou Piniella, it also honors those loyal and patient fans who have stuck by us through thick and thin. We came awfully close to delivering a championship to Chicago in 1969. To this day, my old teammates — Billy Williams, Ron Santo, Randy Hundley, Fergie Jenkins and others — talk about that opportunity that just was not to be.

Wherever I travel around the world, I encounter fans of the Chicago Cubs. I am amazed by their spirit and determination. I am humbled by the many people who tell me that they grew up watching me and the Cubs on good old WGN-TV. The memories for all of us will last forever.

Ernie Banks absorbs the sight of his statue at its unveiling on Opening Day. **CHARLES CHERNEY**

RICK MORRISSEY   A North Side rarity: These guys can play

THEY'RE GOOD, THESE CUBS. Very, very good. If there's an antivenin for what many people believe is a snakebitten franchise, an antidote to 100 years of hard luck, this would be it.

The one thing that ties together the Cubs teams that came before 2008 is the fact that most of them simply weren't very good, or at least weren't good enough. Come to think of it, many of them stunk to high heaven. You can talk about hexes and curses and billy goats all you want — and there's no denying those topics have a suffocating weight to them — but very rarely has the Cubs organization put itself in a position to be a serious contender.

This team is loaded. Any impartial observer, and perhaps even a passing White Sox fan, would have to agree.

Start with the pitching. Ryan Dempster came out of nowhere — OK, the bullpen — to become one of the best starters in the National League. Who saw that coming, besides Dempster?

On the heels of the Brewers acquiring CC Sabathia, Rich Harden arrived in a trade from Oakland and was almost unbeatable.

When the Cubs-Astros series was moved to Milwaukee because of Hurricane Ike, the force of nature known as Carlos Zambrano threw a no-hitter Sept. 14 against Houston.

And here come Carlos Marmol and Kerry Wood out of the bullpen.

Man, you try going up against all of that.

Those "Cubbie occurrences" manager Lou Piniella talks about? Those odd, usually bad things that seem to happen only to the Cubs? When you have a staff with that kind of quality, it negates any of the bizarro-world stuff.

Piniella gets props for keeping this team focused on the prize, but he should thank general manager Jim Hendry — every day — for giving him this roster. If it seemed as if every Cub made the All-Star Game, it's because they did. Didn't they?

A manager can work with a lineup that starts with Alfonso Soriano, Ryan Theriot, Derrek Lee, Aramis Ramirez and Geovany Soto.

First among equals? How about Soto, who should be the National League rookie of the year. His numbers are very good, but his maturity and coolness are exceptional. He was the catcher for Zambrano's no-hitter and when Ted Lilly took a no-hitter into the seventh the next day. That's not all the pitchers' work.

Or maybe Mark DeRosa is the engine that drives this team. He plays several positions, had his best year by far in terms of power numbers and lent a veteran's calmness and leadership to the equation.

Moments? How about Jim Edmonds' two-homer game against St. Louis? Henry Blanco won that game with a hit in the 11th inning. Or Reed Johnson's diving, one-for-the-ages catch against the Nationals, the one that left him with the bill of his cap flipped up like Gomer Pyle's?

The Cubs had that bad losing streak at the end of August and the beginning of September. The team lost eight of nine games, and even though very little was in jeopardy because its division and wild-card leads were so big, Cubs fans couldn't help but fret. When you have a history of disappointment, you're pretty sure more is right around the corner. But the Cubs turned it around almost immediately.

What, you worry?

When he arrived in Chicago before the 2007 season, Piniella talked about putting swagger into Cubs baseball. It seemed like a foreign concept at the time, but it took root. Grown men and women who had known very little success as fans of the Cubs stopped tiptoeing around. At first, it looked a little awkward and uncomfortable. But now?

Strutting like true believers.

Given the history, is it all too good to be true? The strutters won't even deign to answer.

MIKE DOWNEY   Dead wrong, and as happy as can be

WELL, I WAS WRONG about just about everything.

I thought Milwaukee would win the division and the Cubs would be the wild cards.

Wrong. The Brewers went as flat as last year's beer.

I thought Joe Girardi would make a better manager for the Cubs than old-school Lou Piniella would.

Wrong. Joe couldn't even get the Yankees into the playoffs with that zillion-dollar payroll of theirs.

I thought Kosuke Fukudome would have a better rookie year than Geovany Soto would.

Wrong. Fooky never did find his batting eye after Opening Day, and for most of the year Soto turned out to be Joltin' Geo.

I thought Jim Edmonds was done. Washed up. Ready to be put out to pasture.

Wrong. He can still field in center like Willie Mays, and he can still whack a ball out of a park.

I thought Ryan Theriot's batting average would ultimately plunge to, oh, .270, maybe .275.

Wrong. The Riot hovered above .300 practically from beginning to end.

I thought Ryan Dempster might win 10 games, maybe 12.

Wrong. He not only was the Cubs' main man on the mound, he was the one who had the courage to go on record in spring training that This Will Be The Year.

I thought Carlos Zambrano didn't deserve to be called a superstar, never having won 20 games in a season.

Wrong. He delivered the most electrifying performance of the year with his no-hitter, not only when the team needed it most, but at a time when everybody feared he was hurt.

I thought Kerry Wood would be replaced as the closer by Carlos Marmol.

Wrong. He kept everybody on the edges of their seats a few times, but except for one mysterious flesh-eating blister, Wood was there for the Cubs all the way.

I thought Alfonso Soriano would have to be lifted from left field in the eighth inning of every game for a defensive replacement.

Wrong. He hops in the field (as opposed to Sammy Sosa's hops at the plate), but Soriano held his ground and did his job out there more often than not.

I thought Reed Johnson was an OK pickup, nothing more.

Wrong. What an acquisition. The guy hits, he runs,

he's got a great personality ... and he made one of the five best catches I've ever seen.

I thought Mark DeRosa would have a solid, respectable season, nothing more.

Wrong. He might just be this team's MVP. Did it all, played wherever he was put, swung a good bat, showed a ton of class.

I thought Ted Lilly might win, oh, 10, 12 games, absolutely no more.

Wrong. He won a whole bunch more than that. And with the hardest act to follow of 2008, he darn near achieved immortality by following a no-hitter with a no-hitter.

I thought Mike Fontenot would spend most of the year in Iowa.

Wrong. He was extremely valuable, and he even hit more home runs than a lot of larger National Leaguers did.

I thought Jeff Samardzija would be a very valuable pickup — for a team in the NFL.

Wrong. He put Fighting Irish baseball on the map.

I thought the Cubs would win 90 games, no more.

Wrong. They did win 90, but they did it by mid-September.

I thought 2008 at Wrigley Field might end with a "For Sale" sign out front ... or even a foreclosure notice.

Wrong. It was one wild party. See you there again in 2009, beginning with that Blackhawks hockey game.

PHIL ROGERS   Drop prior allegiance — and Prior jerseys

MARK PRIOR IS GONE, but it's going to be a while before he's forgotten, especially if the fans who invested in T-shirts and jerseys bearing his No. 22 keep wearing them to Wrigley Field.

Please stop wearing them. Please follow Cubs general manager Jim Hendry's lead and get rid of them.

It's always painful to throw away an investment, especially one that once made you feel so good about yourself and your team, but enough is enough. Pitch those shirts, just like Hendry did Prior himself.

Get fitted with an '08 model Zambrano jersey or a Harden jersey. If you are a risk-taker, go for the Dempster model. He's eligible for free agency after the season, but it's hard to imagine Hendry letting him escape after his wire-to-wire performance. And you can bet Dempster doesn't want to go anywhere.

You could never be sure with Prior. He seemed a perfect fit for the Cubs in 2003, when he and Kerry Wood took them to the threshold of the World Series, but Prior never seemed quite himself after Florida's eight-run eighth inning in Game 6.

Physically, the 2003 average of 115 pitches per start, most in the majors that season, might have taken a toll on him. Emotionally, he always seemed jumpy, like trouble lurked around every corner he turned at Wrigley Field.

Yet there was no denying Prior's ability. If he could ever get himself healthy and mentally right, the Cubs could still have a dominating starter to put alongside Zambrano in their rotation.

That's what I was thinking when the 2007 season ended with Prior's future in doubt. He had undergone shoulder surgery the previous spring, the first time in his career he'd had an operation, and he projected to get back on the mound at some point in '08. The Cubs had invested more than $14 million in Prior already and could keep him one more year for another $3 million. Surely they would do it, right?

Wrong. Hendry decided to pull the plug.

Some of us thought it was a gamble. It turned out to be the ultimate addition-by-subtraction move.

By cutting ties with Prior, Hendry spared pitching coach Larry Rothschild, trainer Mark O'Neal and others throughout the organization the effort they had been making to get Prior back up to his 2003 standard. He took away the constant tease that Prior's talent provided, making it imperative to assemble real pitching depth, not the best-case-scenario kind of

depth that came with having Prior on the roster.

This was a great move.

"I haven't thought about Mark in a long time," Hendry said late in the season. "At the time, as I said then, it wasn't a difficult decision. It was a disappointing decision. We were admitting that we weren't going to get out of Mark what we thought we were, and that was disappointing for everybody, especially Mark. But in this business there are times you turn the page, and that was one of them."

Maybe the Cubs would have won the Central and made a long playoff run with Prior still hanging around their training room. But Hendry and others had to nod knowingly when Prior reported to camp with the San Diego Padres, supposedly ahead of schedule and talking a good game, and then experienced arm problems.

Prior had his second surgery in two years in July, eliminating any chance he'd pitch this season. His 2009 season and his career are in doubt. But because Hendry had effectively said good riddance, the black cloud didn't hang over the Cubs this time.

Please, fans, no more Prior jerseys at Wrigley Field. They're reminders of one of the most painful chapters in Cubs history, for everyone involved.

PAUL SULLIVAN   An oasis in a desert of failure

IN MY FIRST YEAR as Cubs beat writer for the Tribune, the team set a National League record with 14 straight losses to begin the 1997 season.

Not exactly the way you want to begin a new stretch of your career, knowing your team is already out of contention and you'll be spending the next 5½ months looking ahead to next year.

But even losing teams must be covered from start to finish, so I got through the year unscathed, learning the workings of the organization and hoping for better days ahead.

Little did I realize 1998 would be one of the most exciting years in franchise history. Kerry Wood tied a major-league record with 20 strikeouts in only his fifth start. Sammy Sosa dueled Mark McGwire in an effort to break Roger Maris' single-season home run record. And there was the unmatchable atmosphere of Game 163, when the Cubs beat San Francisco at Wrigley Field to head to the playoffs for the first time since 1989. Sure, the Cubs were swept by Atlanta in the first round of the postseason, but there was no convincing me this wasn't the beginning of a new era.

The Cubs got off to a great start again in '99 and seemed on their way to another postseason appearance. Then Lance Johnson got picked off first to end a game in Arizona, the Cubs came home to get swept by the White Sox and it was all downhill from there.

Manager Jim Riggleman was fired after the season, and soon afterward I was assigned to go back and cover the White Sox. The separation was difficult at first, but baseball is baseball, and it wasn't long before the Cubs were in my rearview mirror.

By the time I returned to the Cubs beat in 2003, things had changed drastically. Genial Jim Hendry had replaced misanthropic Ed Lynch as general manager. Dusty Baker had come over from San Francisco to replace Don Baylor and change the culture of losing. And he did just that, taking the Cubs to the Central Division title in a season so bizarre you'd think it had been scripted by Hunter S. Thompson.

But then came the moment of truth: the double-play ground ball shortstop Alex Gonzalez booted in Game 6 of the National League Championship Series that opened the floodgates to an eight-run eighth inning and sank the Cubs' World Series hopes. An unfortunate fan whose name became synonymous with "Cubbie failures" was ultimately made the scapegoat, letting Gonzalez off the hook. Either way, the Cubs had another chance in Game 7 — and blew it again.

So tough. So Cub.

The 2004 season was a chance for redemption, and newcomers like Derrek Lee, Greg Maddux and Nomar Garciaparra made it the most talented team I had covered. But a final-week collapse after LaTroy Hawkins' implosion at Shea Stadium bounced them out of the playoff picture, and the Cubs reverted to their losing ways in '05.

Baker's final year in '06 was one long nightmare. The final three months were spent speculating on when Baker would get fired as the Cubs finished with the worst record in the National League. That ushered in the Lou Piniella era.

Piniella said things would be different, and they certainly were. After a lethargic April and May, Carlos Zambrano punched Michael Barrett, Piniella kicked dirt on an umpire and the Cubs took off, winning the Central Division. A sweep by Arizona in the postseason wasn't as hard to fathom as the '03 debacle, and Piniella got his players to perform again in '08, breezing to their first back-to-back playoff appearances since 1906-08.

Through good times and bad, covering the Cubs has always been interesting, no matter who was in the dugout or who was running the show. There's something about this team that makes me think it really is the year of the long-awaited happy ending, and all I can do is dream that it doesn't turn out to be just another Cub mirage.

Following page
A vendor's work is never done, not even when the sun is beginning to set at Wrigley Field. **PHIL VELASQUEZ**

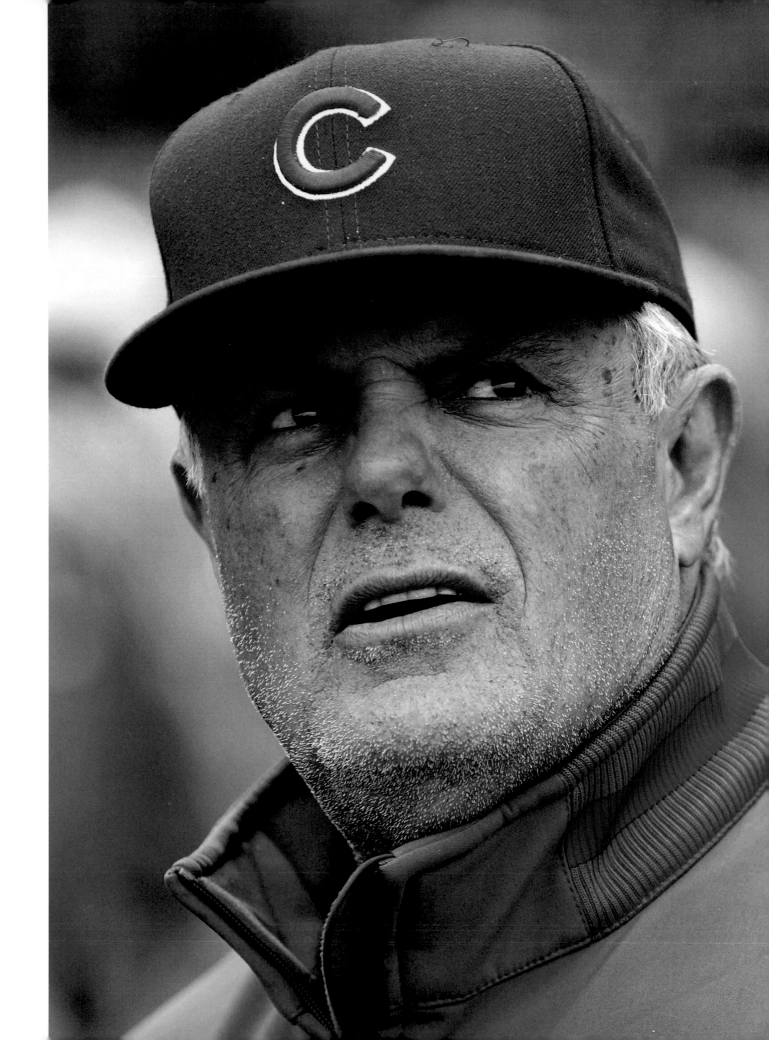

LOU PINIELLA

MANAGER By **PAUL SULLIVAN**

THERE WERE A FEW Cubbie occurrences, a handful of senior moments, a trip to nowhere without a map and a couple of vintage outbursts to liven up the room.

But otherwise it has been a relatively uneventful year for Lou Piniella.

Oh, sure, he proclaimed himself a "rap star" after performing with Ozzie Guillen in a TV commercial, and he got lost driving from Chicago to Cincinnati with first-base coach Matt Sinatro. He informed us he was "not a weatherman" when the Astros lobbied to play the Cubs in Houston before the arrival of Hurricane Ike, and he admitted he used to buy the water coolers he once smashed with regularity.

And, yes, Piniella had his annual YouTube moment early, angrily posing a rhetorical question to a radio reporter who wondered aloud after a game whether the veteran manager had ever considered lifting left fielder Alfonso Soriano for late-inning defense.

"Do you think I'm stupid?" Piniella snapped.

The answer from Cubs fans was a resounding no, that Piniella was in fact a genius who could take the Cubs to the Promised Land.

It didn't take long for Chicago to realize that Piniella was one of the sharpest managers in the franchise's star-crossed history, or that Sweet Lou had the experience, the judgment, the tactical skills and the charisma to ensure a team loaded with star power would meld into one cohesive unit.

It took an entire spring training and two months of the 2007 season before Piniella figured things out and began making the necessary changes to turn around the team. And after a quick exit from the postseason and a few roster adjustments, he transformed the Cubs into the National League's most dominant team in the '08 season.

Piniella insists he has mellowed over the years, though it's obvious the fire inside him has yet to be extinguished.

"He expects execution to be perfect," Mark DeRosa said. "You can't mistake kindness for weakness. I've always felt the manager has to assert himself in some form or fashion, and Lou does a very good job of that.

"Mellow would be the wrong word. I'd say he's more comfortable being around us, as we are being around him."

During the wild and crazy regular season at spring training, there were moments, naturally, that tried Piniella's patience. (Of course, the term "Piniella's patience" is considered an oxymoron by many who know him, but that's a story for another day).

Some of those moments were related to the performance of a player or the team itself, while others could be traced to the unending questions he received regarding the Cubs' well-chronicled history of futility. As much as Piniella loves his job, he has never grown accustomed to the constant skepticism.

"It is work, believe me," he said. "And there are a lot of questions you get asked that you wouldn't necessarily get asked elsewhere."

Most of them this season concerned all things Soriano — his fielding, his little hop before catching a fly ball, his penchant for admiring home runs, and mostly his spot in the batting order. A hot-button topic on radio, in taverns and in the Wrigley Field bleachers after Soriano got off to a slow start, the Soriano questions drove Piniella crazy in April.

"You can ask all you want," he said with a sigh after another early-season postgame grilling. "And you're asking. But I'm telling you, I don't need to justify it. I think I know what I'm doing."

Piniella then started laughing and turned the tables on the questioners, asking why they continued to ask him about where Soriano should hit.

"I've never really had this many questions about lineups," he said. "I think you all fantasize about lineups at night. I really do. It's the damnedest thing. I think you all do too much with this lineup. I think we could pick names out of a hat, and if the guy is swinging the bat well he can hit out of any spot in the lineup, and you win baseball games."

Indeed, Lou Piniella was no "rap star." But he did manage a champion. **PHIL VELASQUEZ**

Ryan Dempster's 2008 success never burst Piniella's bubble. **NUCCIO DINUZZO**

Eventually, Piniella flat-out refused to answer any more questions about Soriano, calling it a "mute story."

When Soriano returned from a broken hand in the second half of the season and resumed hitting home runs, the story went away. Piniella had proved himself again, and the Cubs were rolling along toward a playoff season. They won nine series in a row from late July through August, an accomplishment no Cubs team had achieved since 1907. Piniella once again had to remind

people to avoid "getting giddy," as there was a long way to go before the postseason rotation could be planned.

Then came the inevitable bump. The Cubs lost seven of eight games, and Piniella finally lost it after a 4-3 defeat Sept. 9 in St. Louis. It was full-metal Lou, with all the trimmings. His voice rose as the rant went on, the words spilling over into the empty clubhouse a few feet away.

"I know we're trying," he said. "I've got no

Coaches Matt Sinatro and Alan Trammell flank Piniella during batting practice. **PHIL VELASQUEZ**

complaints with the effort. But you've got to get the job done. We can talk about having fun. We can talk about relaxing. You've got to get your damn shirts rolled up and go out and kick somebody's ass. That's what you've got to do, period."

Piniella picked up a bottle of beer and returned to his cramped office. The message was sent, though few of the players were still around to hear it.

When Ted Lilly, a pitcher, slammed into Cardinals catcher Yadier Molina on a play at the plate the next night, it was a signature moment in a dreamlike season. The Cubs finally had their swagger back.

"He was upset with our team?" a puzzled Lilly asked after being informed of Piniella's rant. "You know, he might be over 100, but he's still got a lot of fire in him."

Lilly was off by some 35 years, but his point had been made.

Piniella would not settle for 90 or more wins if it

meant a mediocre finish, and he challenged his team to play up to its talent level.

The Cubs took the next two games in St. Louis, had an unexpected two-day break caused by Hurricane Ike's assault on Houston, then beat the Astros in a rescheduled series at Miller Park, with Carlos Zambrano throwing a no-hitter and Lilly following with six no-hit innings en route to a one-hitter for him and the bullpen.

They rode the wave to the Central Division title a few days later at Wrigley Field, catching their breath and finishing the regular season strong. Whether Piniella's choreographed performance in the visiting manager's office at Busch Stadium had anything to do with the sudden turnaround is a "mute story," as Lou would say.

The Cubs were on their way to a second straight postseason for the first time since they made three straight World Series appearances from 1906-08, and Piniella was one step closer to finishing the gargantuan task of turning a team with the league's worst record in 2006 into a realistic World Series hopeful.

It was another strange year filled with freak injuries, unforeseen occurrences and moments of sheer madness, but Piniella would want it no other way. He believed all along he would be the one to guide the Cubs to nirvana, and he enjoyed taking Cubs fans on the ride of their lives.

Piniella has managed five major-league teams and enjoyed success in New York, Cincinnati and Seattle before a failed stint in his home area of Tampa Bay. But after figuring out the "Chicago thing," his final managerial job was perhaps his most rewarding. Chicago will always be in his heart, no matter where Piniella winds up.

"It's something that a person is fortunate to experience," he said. "Obviously everyone who comes here has the same thing in mind, and that's to end the drought. But you do the best you can. That's all you can do.

"I'm here basically for the same thing my predecessors were here for, and hopefully I'll have a taste of that success that's eluded some of them. I like managing the Cubs. I enjoy the challenge, the atmosphere I work in, and I do the best I can. But remember, after this job, I'm not looking for any more. I'm going to go home and watch Cubs baseball on WGN, just like everybody else."

Piniella gets up close and personal with umpire Rob Drake, who ejected him. **SCOTT STRAZZANTE**

JIM HENDRY
GENERAL MANAGER

THE ARCHITECT OF THE 2008 CUBS, general manager Jim Hendry, discusses with Tribune baseball reporter Phil Rogers how he put the team together.

Armed with a quick wit and a steady trigger finger, Jim Hendry is the first executive in the modern era to get the Cubs into the playoffs in three seasons.

Hendry, in his 14th year in the organization and his seventh as general manager, rebuilt his lineup on the fly in 2003, adding Aramis Ramirez, Kenny Lofton and Randall Simon in midseason trades. He set the tone for the division championship in '07 by bringing in Lou Piniella to replace Dusty Baker and signing Alfonso Soriano to highlight an off-season spending spree, then dumped one of his personal favorites, catcher Michael Barrett, when his ability behind the plate deteriorated.

This time around Hendry took a team widely picked as the National League favorite and made it even stronger with a deal for Rich Harden and the shrewd signing of discards Jim Edmonds and Reed Johnson. He knows nothing is guaranteed in October, but he'll take his chances with the Lou Crew. In mid-September, he got off his cell phone long enough to discuss the 2008 Cubs.

Top, Jim Hendry (center, back to camera) answers questions from the media. **PHIL VELASQUEZ** For team pix

Far left, Hendry mugs as the Cubs' brass gets together for a group photo. **PHIL VELASQUEZ**

Left, Hendry strikes a thoughtful pose at the front of the dugout. **BONNIE TRAFELET**

Hendry is ecstatic on July 8. You would be, too, if you'd just acquired Rich Harden. **SCOTT STRAZZANTE**

Following page
From spring training right through the regular season, the Cubs were on a mission. **PHIL VELASQUEZ**

What's your general philosophy on team-building?
HENDRY "You always like to start with a deep pitching staff. You want to feel like you have a good rotation and good relievers. A dependable bullpen gives you a chance to have a competitive club. You're not going to go on many long losing streaks. Coming into the year, I wanted to make sure I had six or seven starters — good pitchers, and depth. If you have that, you're going to win your share of close games. It always starts with that."

What else were you looking to change after getting swept by Arizona in the playoffs last year?
HENDRY "I was looking to add depth to our bench. We've been fortunate because we have had a lot of parts in our [farm] system. I've got to give credit to Lou. He does a good job playing guys when they come up. He puts 'em right in there, and not many managers do that. That's important. Guys get called up because they're going good, and if they don't play, they're not going good anymore. In building the lineup, our priority was to play better defense. We wanted to get a left-handed hitter in the outfield, and we did that with [Kosuke] Fukudome. Once we got him, we really thought we were in good shape."

The Cubs scored only six runs in the three playoff games last year. Did that leave you wanting a left-handed hitter to balance out Soriano, Ramirez and Derrek Lee?
HENDRY "No. We faced three good pitchers, and they shut us down. Lee, Ramirez and Soriano, they've had very good careers, very good years, and they didn't hit in the playoffs last year. They were obviously a big factor in getting there. They're all right-handed, but that's not something you worry about. I guess if you could take one of them and make him left-handed, well, that might be better. But I just thought it wouldn't hurt to have a left-handed hitter because we were also looking at a lineup with [Geovany] Soto, [Ryan] Theriot and [Mark] DeRosa, all of whom are right-handed hitters."

Did you look for a No. 2 starter type, like Harden, in the off-season?
HENDRY "No. We thought Rich Hill was going to be a 13- or 14-game winner. That's one thing that didn't happen. Everybody knows how I feel about Ryan Dempster. I don't want to say I told you so, but I was very confident that he was going to do a good job moving out of the bullpen and into the rotation. I can't say I knew he was going to go to the All-Star Game and win [almost 20] games, but I knew he was going to get the job done. I don't deserve any credit for that; he does."

When did you start thinking about adding a starter?
HENDRY "Hill did not start well for us. It was clear to all of us that we've got a really good club, that we have a chance to go a long way, and that [adding a starter] would help us get in [the playoffs] and ... help us in the postseason. We only called about two pitchers, [CC] Sabathia and Harden. We got one. Doug Melvin [the Milwaukee GM] got the other."

Was the Harden trade a response to the Brewers getting Sabathia?
HENDRY "No. I had been working on that for three weeks before it got done. We had talked about CC, too, but everybody knew [Cleveland GM] Mark Shapiro wanted one bat in the deal who he felt could be a difference-maker. I don't think he felt we had one of those, so we were going to have trouble doing that. I think we knew on a Sunday that Milwaukee was going to get Sabathia, and we got Harden a day later. ... We just wanted another arm, and Harden had been the guy we wanted."

How important has Geovany Soto been? Did you feel he was a risk coming into the season?
HENDRY "Very important. One of the most important players. He came to camp in '07 and opened eyes. Then he worked hard to get in great shape, and he went out and was the MVP in the [Pacific Coast League], the first catcher to do that since [Mike] Piazza. We brought him up to the big leagues, and he handled it in September. He swung the bat well and worked with the pitchers. We really felt good about him. Plus Henry [Blanco] was healthy. We felt good at catcher."

What scouts have had a big impact on this team?
HENDRY "Mark Servais in spring training, on Reed Johnson. I was getting mad at myself. We had talked about finding a free-agent center fielder to take the load off [Felix] Pie. November came and went, December came and went, January came and went, and I was sitting there with nobody. Mark Servais was working Florida, and he kept calling about Reed Johnson. ... He had an idea that with Shannon Stewart there, [the Blue Jays] wouldn't keep Johnson. One week Reed played three or four games in a row in center, and Mark called and said, 'If they let him go, he'd be great for us.' [Scouting director] Tim Wilken had his cell number and called him 15 minutes after Toronto let him go. I was on the phone with his agents, and we knew right away that if he cleared waivers he'd be a Cub. That situation really worked out well."

CHAPTER 1

Getting ready

By **PAUL SULLIVAN**

THE 2008 CUBS BEGAN to take shape on a cold December day in 2007 when Japanese star Kosuke Fukudome agreed to a $48 million deal the same night Mark Prior was not tendered a contract.

A new day dawned for the Cubs with their entry into the Japanese free-agent market and the shedding of a one-time star who had turned into an albatross with his inability to stay healthy.

But the bulk of the winter was spent waiting for a man who never arrived. Trade talks with Baltimore for second baseman Brian Roberts continued throughout spring training, making Roberts a talk-radio topic in Chicago for nearly four agonizing months.

When the Cubs reported to Mesa, Ariz., for spring training in February, all the pieces were in place for a solid season. Ryan Dempster, Jason Marquis and Jon Lieber were supposedly competing for two spots in the rotation, with Carlos Zambrano, Ted Lilly and Rich Hill assured of the other three. Kerry Wood, Bob Howry and Carlos Marmol were supposedly competing for Dempster's old role as closer.

The rest of the positions were set, with rookie Geovany Soto behind the plate, Mark DeRosa cemented at second barring a trade for Roberts and Felix Pie getting another chance to win the center-field job, vying with Sam Fuld.

The Cubs were almost everyone's pick to win the Central Division, and many were picking them to go to the World Series and even win it. The pressure was on from the outset, unlike Lou Piniella's first year at the helm in 2007, when spring training was more of a feeling-out period.

"It doesn't make me nervous," Piniella said. "It's flattering. I think it's probably an in-vogue thing to pick the Cubs because of the 100th year, but we've got to play on the field. It's flattering that people look at our club and like it. But it doesn't put any pressure on me."

Spring training started with a bang when Dempster announced "I think we're going to win the World Series" even before walking through the clubhouse door on the day pitchers and catchers reported.

It got a little scary when DeRosa was carted out of

Kosuke Fukudome attended his first spring training as a Cub. **PHIL VELASQUEZ**

Alex Cintron (left), Sam Fuld, Jake Fox and Micah Hoffpauir put cleats to turf at camp. **PHIL VELASQUEZ**

camp on a stretcher and underwent surgery for an irregular heartbeat, and it turned a little strange when reliever Jose Ascanio was punched in the eye while sitting in his car at a convenience store.

Marquis popped off that he wanted to be a starter or go "elsewhere," to which Piniella replied, "Let him go." Piniella apologized, and Marquis wound up as the fifth

starter anyway. Pie twisted one of his testicles in the most painful injury of the spring, while Wood suffered through back spasms, Alfonso Soriano broke a bone in his middle finger and Scott Eyre couldn't pitch one day because of "itchy feet."

It was all so Cublike, the kind of stuff Piniella referred to as "Cubbie occurrences."

The Cubs managed to get through the spring with no major disasters, focusing on preparing for a season that was already being celebrated as the centennial: the 100th anniversary of their last title.

"How do I view it? I mentioned 100 years because that's all I hear," Piniella said. "It's not something I came up with, believe me. I don't know how I view it. It seems rather improbable. I mean, that's a long time. Let's see if we can do something about it. That's all we can do. We're going to try our darnedest to do it."

Six months later, the Cubs were in the playoffs and ready to take the next big step. The journey that began in February in Arizona was about to end, but no one who went through it would ever forget the ride.

Coaches Larry Rothschild and Matt Sinatro join players Bob Howry, J.D. Closser and Mike Fontenot to watch Kerry Wood pitch at camp in Mesa, Ariz. **PHIL VELASQUEZ**

CHAPTER 2

The first half By **DAVE VAN DYCK**

AS THE CUBS FINISHED spring training, manager Lou Piniella's parting words were, "It's important to get off to a good start."

So how did the Cubs begin the regular season?

They lost their first two games to the Brewers — at Wrigley Field, no less. That qualified as anything but good, considering the Central Division was expected to be a head-to-head battle between the Cubs and Milwaukee.

But by the All-Star break, partying had replaced panic, Wrigley Field had been converted into a consecrated cathedral full of blue-background "W" flags and the daily sellout crowd was singing a chorus of "Go, Cubs, Go."

Those first two games were the only time in the first half the Cubs lost two straight home games, and by the time a National League-record eight Cubs had become All-Stars, their lead was up to 4½ games over the Cardinals and their 57-38 record matched the Angels for best in baseball.

It was their best first half since, gulp, 1969.

"Once this team started to win with more regularity, it got more confident," Piniella said. "Confidence has a whole lot to do with winning and losing games."

Said general manager Jim Hendry: "I see a real team. I see guys pulling for each other and overcoming injuries and keeping the losing streaks short. And I see a lot of guys who care more about winning than their own individual accolades or numbers."

Hendry himself contributed to the first-half success by plucking center fielders Reed Johnson and Jim Edmonds off the waiver wire and bringing in starter Rich Harden right before the trading deadline.

All of them provided magical moments, with Edmonds hitting his 10th home run in Harden's debut on July 12, an 8-7 extra-inning victory over the Giants. In a preview of things to come, Harden threw 5⅓ scoreless innings and struck out 10.

Everything seemed to work in the first half, especially at Wrigley Field.

The Cubs avenged their playoff loss of the previous October by sweeping the Diamondbacks on May 9-11. They swept the White Sox in an emotion-filled series

June 20-22. They won 22 of 26 games during four May and June homestands, including seven straight come-from-behind victories.

The statistics were beginning to stack up to show that this would be a special season. So were the mounting mass of memories.

Of course, there were plenty of "Cubbie occurrences," as Piniella liked to call strange happenings. For instance, the Mother's Day victory over the Diamondbacks was beset by rain that made it a muddy track and hungry seagulls that invaded the outfield.

And there were plenty of heroes, one for almost every victory.

During their hottest stretch in May, the Cubs got consecutive wins from Sean Gallagher, Bob Howry, Michael Wuertz, Scott Eyre and Ryan Dempster.

Newcomer Kosuke Fukudome became an instant celebrity for right-field bleacher fans who had so admired Sammy Sosa and Andre Dawson. Fukudome's statistics — .384 on-base percentage, seven homers and 36 RBIs — were rewarded with a fan vote to start the All-Star Game. And rookie catcher Geovany Soto was an All-Star for his 16 homers and 56 RBIs.

While the offense did its part, the plan to switch roles for Ryan Dempster and Kerry Wood worked nearly to perfection.

Dempster lost on the last day before the break, giving him a 10-1 record at Wrigley Field, and Wood had saved 24 games. Symbolically, the two — Dempster as the starter and Wood as the closer —teamed up for the first victory of the season, April 3 against Milwaukee.

The best news was that both were relatively healthy at the break, despite being in unfamiliar positions, though Wood missed the All-Star Game with a pesky blister on his index finger.

"I feel strong," Dempster said, shrugging off concerns that his arm couldn't hold up through the

Rookie catcher Geovany Soto was one of the best early surprises. **PHIL VELASQUEZ**

Derrek Lee homers, Ryan Theriot scores and all is well in Cub land. **PHIIL VELASQUEZ**

grind of starting. "I feel I can keep it going. As a team we should be really proud of ourselves and what we've done."

But health was a concern for the Cubs in the first half. Leadoff man Alfonso Soriano and staff ace Carlos Zambrano spent time on the disabled list, which made the team's record even more remarkable.

"You have to be satisfied," Piniella said at the break. "There were a lot of adversities to overcome. And the team still functioned and held its own."

As it turns out, the first half was only a preview of things to come. Piniella might have had an inkling when he said: "We've been rewarded with a first-place finish at the first half. You hope in the end you're on top."

Following pages
48-49 Reed Johnson catches Chris Iannetta's fly in a 5-4 win over Colorado on May 31, and Kosuke Fukudome backs him up. **BONNIE TRAFELET**

50-51 A reception committee awaits Aramis Ramirez at the plate after his home run beat the White Sox on June 20. **PHIL VELASQUEZ**

Alfonso Soriano is mobbed by Mark DeRosa (top) and Ryan Theriot after his base hit beat the Dodgers 2-1 in 10 innings May 28. **NUCCIO DINUZZO**

CHAPTER 3

The City Series By **DAN McGRATH**

THE CUBS-WHITE SOX "Red Line Series" is always among the high points of any Chicago baseball season, no matter where the teams sit in the standings. The best evidence: Each team had won 30 games in the 11-year history of the rivalry entering this season. And each had scored 291 runs.

This year's renewal brought a special level of excitement. For the first time in series history, both teams were in first place in their divisions when they squared off in Round 1 at Wrigley Field beginning June 20. It seemed fitting that the beyond-capacity crowd was treated to a spine-tingling thriller in the opener.

Pugnacious Sox catcher A.J. Pierzynski was in character and in the middle of things, staking young John Danks to a 3-1 lead with a two-run homer off Ted Lilly in the third inning. But the Cubs placed a timely call to Dr. Long Ball and tied the game when Derrek

Left, fans cheer as Eric Patterson heads for home against the Sox. Above, Brian Marquardt and Brad Schlesh taunt Sox fan Al Julius with brooms before the Cubs finished the sweep at Wrigley Field. **SCOTT STRAZZANTE**

Lee and Aramis Ramirez hit back-to-back homers off Octavio Dotel in the seventh. Ramirez then won it with a walk-off shot off Scott Linebrink, turning the home-plate area into a mosh pit as his jubilant teammates celebrated.

"Our big boys got the job done," manager Lou Piniella said.

The Cubs continued swinging for the fences — and reaching them — in Game 2, tying a franchise record with four home runs in a nine-run fourth inning that carried them to an 11-7 victory. Two of the homers came from Jim Edmonds, the former Cardinal whose stylish center-field play and awakening bat had rapidly transformed him from Wrigley Field villain to hero.

The red-hot Ramirez and Mike Fontenot also homered for the Cubs, who collected 15 hits.

Wrigley fans broke out the brooms for Sunday's series finale and were not disappointed as the Cubs rolled to a sweep-completing 7-1 victory behind Ryan

Dempster, who was looking more at home at Wrigley Field in 2008 than the familiar ivy on the outfield walls.

Eric Patterson's first major-league homer and Ramirez's fourth in three games were the big hits. Ramirez also contributed two fielding gems at third base.

"Just doing my job," he said with a shrug after the Cubs had swept the Sox for the first time since 2004 and had run their Wrigley Field winning streak to 14 games.

"We're obviously playing with a lot of confidence," Piniella said.

That confidence would be put to the test just one week later, when the Sox retaliated with their own sweep at U.S. Cellular Field.

Nick Swisher hit a grand slam as the Sox rocked Dempster for seven runs in the third inning of Game 1, cruising to a 10-3 victory. Carlos Quentin had four hits and Jermaine Dye drove in three runs.

Aramis Ramirez's game-winning homer June 20 has Chris Dimit fired up. **TERRENCE ANTONIO JAMES**

Game 2 was another tight one, the Sox winning 6-5 on Quentin's solo homer off Carlos Marmol in the seventh. Lee went 5-for-5 for the Cubs, leading off the ninth inning with his fifth hit, a double. But Sox closer Bobby Jenks stranded him at third as the tying run, retiring Ramirez and Edmonds on grounders.

It was Sox fans' turn to haul out the brooms for Game 3, and they were waving them from the second inning on after Piniella was ejected for the first time in 2008 for disputing a call on a checked swing. The manager's dust-up had no effect on the Cubs, who went quietly 5-1 as Brian Anderson, Jim Thome and Quentin slugged homers and Mark Buehrle won his fourth straight game.

Thus the "city title" went unresolved for another year, which was fine with the Cubs and the Sox. They were eager to move on. They had bigger challenges ahead.

Jim Edmonds smiles after his second homer in the fourth inning June 21. **PHIL VELASQUEZ**

Aramis Ramirez points skyward after belting his fourth homer in the three-game series at Wrigley.
SCOTT STRAZZANTE

Preparations are made for the All-Star home run derby at Yankee Stadium. **PHIL VELASQUEZ**

CHAPTER 4

The All-Star Cubs

By **MELISSA ISAACSON**

GEOVANY SOTO LAUGHED when asked how it felt to be the only Puerto Rican-born player at the All-Star Game.

"The whole island is going to be looking at me," Soto said before the 79th Midsummer Classic. "It's unbelievable."

He could have added the city of Chicago as well, as Cubs fans were treated to a staggering eight of their favorite boys in blue on the National League All-Star roster.

"I'm proud that they've played very well and earned this recognition," said manager Lou Piniella, an NL

coach for the game. "We have a large contingent. It speaks of our record, how we've played as a team and how they've played as individuals."

In addition to Soto, Kosuke Fukudome (who went 0-for-2), Aramis Ramirez (walked), Ryan Dempster (struck out the side in the ninth), Carlos Zambrano (gave up one hit in two innings) and Carlos Marmol (struck out two in one inning) were also on the NL squad. Kerry Wood and Alfonso Soriano made the team but did not play due to injuries.

And though Soto went 0-for-2, the moment was truly special for him as the first rookie catcher to start

Cubs All-Stars Geovany Soto, Carlos Marmol (third from left), Alfonso Soriano and Aramis Ramirez are loving the home run derby. **PHIL VELASQUEZ**

an All-Star Game for the National League. He joined countryman Sandy Alomar Jr. as the only rookie All-Star starting catchers, Alomar having done so for Cleveland in 1990.

But it's hard to think of Soto as a rookie. He developed into one of the top catchers in the game over his first full season, an offensive and defensive force whose true value can be measured by the fact that he got stronger as the season wore on.

As most catchers wore down, Soto made 124 starts through August, behind only Russell Martin of the Dodgers and Jason Kendall of the Brewers. He was named rookie of the month in the season's warmest month after batting .355 with five doubles, three homers and 21 RBIs in August. He also walked 13 times and scored 17 runs.

Before 2008, Soto had had only one other 120-game season in his pro career, when he played on the Triple-A and major-league levels in '07. But he refused to give in to fatigue.

"I've got four months to rest [in the off-season]," he said.

Soto made headlines for his offensive output Aug. 26 in Pittsburgh when he drove in seven runs with a home run and two three-run doubles in a 14-9 Cubs victory. It was the first time a Cubs player had amassed seven RBIs in a game since Ramirez did it in September 2006.

But it is Soto's maturity behind the plate and leadership skills that have drawn the most praise.

Cubs TV analyst Bob Brenly, a former catcher, tells the story of Soto sticking his head into Piniella's office last year during the division-clinching celebration and informing him that "in a couple of years, I'm going to be your captain."

Confidence distinguishes Soto from his peers, along with a rocket arm and steady improvement behind the plate and as a hitter.

Soto moved with his family from Puerto Rico to New York as a youngster, learning to speak English in the Bronx. The family eventually settled in Ocala, Fla., then returned to Puerto Rico when Geovany was 8.

Soto said he grew up watching Puerto Rican stars such as Ivan Rodriguez, Bernie Williams, Jorge Posada, Ruben Sierra, the Molina brothers and the

All-Star Geovany Soto takes his place behind the plate at Yankee Stadium. **PHIL VELASQUEZ**

Right, Kerry Wood cradles his son, who cranes his neck for a better view. **PHIL VELASQUEZ**

Alomar brothers. Soto's father, Antonio, dreamed of a major-league career for his son and worked with him tirelessly.

"For me, it's [about] how I was brought up by my parents," Soto said. "It feels very good to give that back, that joy that, 'Hey, Mom and Dad, I made the All-Star team. I owe it all to you.' It feels good for me to say that to my parents and give them that joy that their son is doing so well."

Drafted by the Cubs in the 11th round in 2001, Soto was promoted to the big-league team when rosters expanded Sept. 1, 2007, after an MVP season in the Triple-A Pacific Coast League. He made an immediate impact, hitting .426 in 47 at-bats and earning a spot on the postseason roster. Piniella played Soto ahead of the veteran Kendall in the division series, and he hit the Cubs' only homer of the postseason in Game 2 of Arizona's three-game sweep.

"My whole life I was programmed to be a baseball player," Soto said. "I was a good student, good with numbers and in history. I could have been a lawyer or an accountant. But I had no desire to be anything but a baseball player."

And that he is.

Carlos Zambrano whirls on a pickoff move with Ichiro Suzuki on first. **PHIL VELASQUEZ**

Left, Ryan Dempster holds a camera as his son joins him on the field at the home run derby. **PHIL VELASQUEZ**

Kosuke Fukudome and his son take in the atmosphere at Yankee Stadium.
PHIL VELASQUEZ

Fans are up in arms, but in a good way, as All-Star Aramis Ramirez launches a three-run homer in the Cubs' 3-1 win over the Giants on July 11.
PHIL VELASQUEZ

CHAPTER 5

4 days in Milwaukee

By **DAN McGRATH**

THE MILWAUKEE BREWERS insisted they were an older, wiser, tougher team than the frustrated bunch that looked on helplessly as the Cubs rolled past them to the NL Central title in 2007. They circled a four-game series against the Cubs in late July at Miller Park and eyed it as their opportunity to prove that point. Then they went out and obtained CC Sabathia, the reigning American League Cy Young Award winner, in a daring midseason trade to strengthen a pitching staff headed by the formidable but fragile Ben Sheets.

And it was all for naught.

Playing before four consecutive sellout crowds that included the usual sizable contingent of Cubs fans, the Cubs gave the Brew Crew the back of their hand, sweeping the series with a finality that sent a message of their own: Not this year, fellas.

Game 1 was a taut 6-4 thriller that the Cubs won with RBI hits by Derrek Lee and Mark DeRosa off Brewers closer Salomon Torres in the ninth inning. But the play of the game might well have been a slide.

Trailing 3-2 in the seventh, the Cubs loaded the bases with one out, only to have Lee chop a bouncer to Brewers shortstop J.J. Hardy, a perfect double-play ball. But Reed Johnson hustled down the basepath and took out second baseman Rickie Weeks as he was pivoting, forcing an errant throw that allowed the tying and go-ahead runs to score.

"D-Lee gets an RBI, but Johnson ought to get one too," Cubs TV analyst Bob Brenly said.

Sabathia started for the Brewers, but he didn't figure in the decision.

Milwaukee turned to Sheets in Game 2, and he was no match for Carlos Zambrano, chased during a five-run sixth inning that lifted the Cubs to a 7-1 victory. They strafed Sheets and the Brewers' bullpen for seven straight hits in the inning, Kosuke Fukudome's two-run

triple the biggest. Aramis Ramirez had three doubles among his four hits, and Mark DeRosa drove in two runs.

Zambrano, though, was the story, blanking the Brewers over eight innings on 118 pitches and striking out nine with a dazzling array of pitches.

"His ball was cutting, sinking, moving everywhere," Milwaukee's Mike Cameron said. "He was having fun out there. I think he was making up pitches."

Zambrano left Game 3 starter Ryan Dempster a tough act to follow. But he gave it a shot, limiting the Brewers to a run over seven innings and striking out nine in a 7-2 victory. Ryan Theriot, Alfonso Soriano and Johnson collected three hits apiece as the Cubs banged out 14.

A diving Rickie Weeks gets doubled off first base as Derrek Lee barely beats him to the bag with the throw from the outfield in the Cubs' win July 31. **NUCCIO DINUZZO**

That set the stage for a sweep, and newcomer Rich Harden made it happen, with a big assist from fellow first-year Cub Jim Edmonds. Harden pitched seven innings of one-run ball for his first win as a Cub, and Edmonds slammed two home runs, including a fourth-inning grand slam, as the Cubs cruised 11-4 to complete their first series sweep in Milwaukee in five years. They outscored the Brewers 31-11.

"Milwaukee was playing really good baseball, and we came in here and took it to them," manager Lou Piniella said.

The Brewers grew so frustrated that pitcher Eric Gagne was ejected in the ninth inning of the final game for throwing a pitch behind Edmonds. The Cubs scoffed at the ill-tempered gesture. They had done their talking on the field.

"We're just concerned with playing each game one at a time," Dempster said, "and hopefully at the end we can do something special that hasn't been done in Chicago in a long time."

Left, A four-game sweep in Milwaukee has Jim Edmonds ready to celebrate. **NUCCIO DINUZZO**

Right, Carlos Marmol lets out a shout after getting the last out in Game 1 of the series. **NUCCIO DINUZZO**

Opposite page, it's a three-man mosh pit of Alfonso Soriano, Reed Johnson and Kosuke Fukudome after the Game 3 victory. **NUCCIO DINUZZO**

CHAPTER 6

The stretch drive By **DAN McGRATH**

THE OFT-QUOTED observation that it would take an act of God to get the Cubs to a World Series was always regarded as harmless hyperbole ... until this year.

Hurricane Ike forced a delay and then a transfer of a critical late-season series between the Cubs and the Houston Astros. There's little doubt the disruption of the schedule worked to the Cubs' advantage, not to diminish in any way the human suffering the storm caused as it ravaged the Texas Gulf Coast region with devastating power.

The Cubs had just endured their roughest stretch of the year with seven losses in eight games, five of them at home, where they had been practically unbeatable. Manager Lou Piniella decided some tough love was in order after a listless 4-3 loss Sept. 9 in St. Louis and pointedly reminded his team it was time to "get your damn shirt rolled up and kick somebody's ass."

Ted Lilly — a pitcher, mind you — took Piniella at his word, barreling hard into Cardinals catcher Yadier Molina on a tag play at the plate the next evening. Lilly was out, but his macho maneuver seemed to snap the Cubs out of their lethargy, and they went on to win 4-3.

The next evening's series finale crackled with playoff intensity and ended with high drama: Kerry Wood retired fearsome Albert Pujols on a short fly to center with two runners on to nail down a 3-2 Cubs victory.

Rich Harden, the sensational midseason acquisition from Oakland, got the win, his fifth in six decisions with the Cubs.

With a bit of their swagger restored, the Cubs were scheduled to head for Houston, where the hottest team in the league awaited them. The Astros had won nine of their previous 10 games, including a three-game sweep at Wrigley Field, the first and only one by a Cubs opponent all season.

But Hurricane Ike had other ideas. The Friday and Saturday games were postponed as the Houston area battened down. Then two games moved to Milwaukee, where Miller Park and its roof offered a refuge from the storm and a home away from home to Carlos Zambrano.

Pitching on 11 days' rest necessitated by a balky shoulder, Zambrano threw a no-hitter against the Astros, the Cubs' first since September 1972, when Milt Pappas no-hit the San Diego Padres. Zambrano was in total command, walking one batter, hitting one, striking out 10 and allowing only two balls to leave the infield in the game of his life.

"I'm back," Big Z declared after his 5-0 victory.

So were the Cubs. Lilly nearly matched Zambrano with six no-hit innings at Miller Park the next day, and the Astros managed only one hit in a 9-1 loss, the Cubs becoming the first team in major-league history to follow up a no-hitter with a one-hitter. More importantly, Derrek Lee ended a 150-at-bat power outage with a two-run homer.

Cubs fans being Cubs fans, that slump had touched off something approaching panic. But the rough patch couldn't erase the nice lead the team had built with six months of solid baseball. The Cubs led the league in hitting and scoring for most of the season, and their pitchers ranked second in ERA. They won nine straight series at one point, for the first time in more than 100 years, they compiled the NL's best overall record. And they were nearly invincible at home, with a winning percentage near .680 and losing just three series.

They never lost their flair for the dramatic. Returning to Wrigley after their excellent Miller Park adventure, they kicked the Brewers to the NL Central curb by winning two of three, 5-4 the first night when Wood froze Prince Fielder with a nasty, knee-buckling breaking ball, striking him out to end it with runners at second and third. Fielder had slugged homers in his previous two at-bats.

Two days later the Cubs trailed 6-2 in the ninth when Geovany Soto capped a four-run rally with a three-run homer to force extra innings. After Wood wriggled free from a second-and-third, nobody-out predicament in the 12th, Lee won it with an RBI single.

"Heck of a ballgame, uplifting to us and deflating to the other team," Piniella said. "That's the beauty of baseball. You never know what you have until that last out."

The Cubs knew what they had — a division championship, their second straight and third in six years.

The bandwagon was gassed up and ready to roll.

The Cubs' win Sept. 15 at Miller Park indeed was priceless for Zoe Troxell, 6, of Peoria. **NUCCIO DINUZZO**

Jim Edmonds answers a curtain call after his second solo home run in a 3-2 victory Aug. 8 against the Cardinals. **PHIL VELASQUEZ**

Opposite page, Mark DeRosa turns to watch Alfonso Soriano's homer, which drove him in Aug. 5 against Houston.
PHIL VELASQUEZ

Top, a fan gets in on the fun by slapping hands with Aramis Ramirez.
BONNIE TRAFELET

Ryan Theriot, Bob Howry and DeRosa get an early start on the official team photo.
PHIL VELASQUEZ

Carlos Zambrano, naturally, is the center of attention after his no-hitter against the Astros on Sept. 14. **NUCCIO DINUZZO**

Left fielder Alfonso Soriano runs down Austin Kearns' deep fly in a loss to Washington on Aug. 22.
PHIL VELASQUEZ

The transition from starter to closer is a challenge Kerry Wood is handling well. **PHIL VELASQUEZ**

34 KERRY WOOD

Steve Rosenbloom chats with the flame-throwing closer

I'D LOVE TO START. But I'm realistic about the fact that I probably won't be doing that again. I've taken a liking to the role I'm in and take pride in doing what I'm doing.

THE BIGGEST SURPRISE is no matter how you feel that day, good or bad — especially bad, if you're not feeling as good as you want to feel — once you get into the game and that adrenaline kicks in, it's amazing what adrenaline can do for you. I mean, at times you have to step off and try to catch your breath and control it.

I WAS AN HOUR AWAY from calling Jim (1) and saying, "I'm sorry, but it's done." (2) Then I talked to my physical therapist and went out and played catch one more time just to see before I made the phone call. I went out and threw and said, "I can't believe this. My arm feels great." My therapist was like, "Why don't we wait to make that phone call until tomorrow?" I said, "OK, we'll see how it feels when I come in." I came in the next day and felt better than I did the day before. So we never made the phone call.

Wood and catcher Henry Blanco have that winning feeling. **PHIL VELASQUEZ**

I FEEL LIKE we've got more depth top to bottom, from first starter to last starter, from long guy to closer. I think we have enough pieces to get the job done. Quality pieces.

HONESTLY, the '03 lineup was good, but this is a dominating lineup from top to bottom. Even when you double-switch in the seventh inning and put in Fontenot, guys say, "Who's this Fontenot guy?" He's got about 10 homers and driven in 40-something runs off the bench. In every aspect of the game, we have depth.

I'M ONE OF THE GUYS not comfortable talking about it because it's a long ways away (3). I've had this "C" on my chest for 10 years now. I know how it goes.

I HATE TO PUT IT ON BARTMAN, but that's the first thing that comes to mind. I think for anybody in Cub Nation, that's the first thing they think of.

ROUNDING FIRST BASE and turning to second and looking into the bleachers and seeing cups and beer flying everywhere — that was probably one of the coolest moments I've ever been a part of. (4)

NOLAN RYAN. Just the way he went about his business and the way he was able to dominate a game and take it over.

I REMEMBER a couple days before I was getting asked about it (5), and I said, "I'm disappointed that I'm not going to be able to see him get his 300th win." Then I remember thinking, "I'd better go beat him so I don't have to see it and eat my words."

WE GO INTO CINCINNATI, Milwaukee, St. Louis, we go into the hotel, and there's 150 Cubs fans in there screaming when we come in. It's crazy. I'm staying on the 16th floor and get on the elevator, and we stop four times along the way, and the door opens and there are 10 Cubs fans waiting for someone to get out on that floor.

I'VE HAD OPPORTUNITIES to leave Chicago and go other places. Obviously, I love Chicago, and they've been great to me and my family. The fans have been great. The organization has been great to me. But I dread leaving here and having them win it the next year. You put all the time in, you've been on some good teams and some bad teams — it's bound to happen eventually. I might as well stay here as long as I can and hopefully be a part of it.

IF WE EVER WON the World Series in Chicago, I would need a helicopter to pick me up and get me out of here right after the game.

1—Cubs general manager Jim Hendry. 2—While rehabbing from a partly torn rotator cuff diagnosed in 2006. 3—The World Series. 4—His home run against Florida in Game 7 of the National League Championship Series. 5—His 2003 start against Yankees pitcher Roger Clemens at Wrigley Field.

46 RYAN DEMPSTER

Brutal off-season workouts pay off for new starter   By **DAVE VAN DYCK**

SPRING TRAINING BEGAN with a bang, with a bold prediction from Ryan Dempster that the Cubs would win the World Series.

The prophecy earned Dempster the nickname "Madame Cleo" for his supposed psychic skills.

And while purists and black-cat theorists may have cringed, teammate Derrek Lee thought it appropriate for a team that had been pushed from the playoffs in three games the previous year.

"I like him saying that," Lee said. "That, obviously, is our goal."

As if to back up his words, Dempster pitched the Cubs to their first victory of the season, a reassuring Wrigley Field win over Milwaukee on April 3. He also pitched the Cubs within two victories of clinching another Central Division title while handing Milwaukee's CC Sabathia his first loss Sept. 16 at Wrigley Field.

For a guy known more for his stand-up comedy than his stance on the future and for a guy making the retransformation from closer to starter, Dempster became the spiritual and physical leader of a team that adopted his tenacity.

It is a side of Dempster that few see, because behind that carefree exterior is a ferocious competitor, one unafraid of jumping back into a starting role for the first time since 2003 with Cincinnati.

The transition couldn't have happened without the consent of general manager Jim Hendry, who had known Dempster for more than a decade and had sought him after elbow surgery in late 2003 because of that knowledge.

"You get to know somebody, and it becomes a character thing," Hendry said. "He's a great teammate, very driven to do it and do it well."

So Hendry signed off on role reversals for Dempster and Kerry Wood, even though Hendry insists "Demp

Known as a great teammate, Dempster shares a laugh with Ted Lilly. **BONNIE TRAFELET**

did an excellent job closing for us."

Hendry, through Dempster, was rewarded with an All-Star appearance, Dempster striking out the side in the ninth to send the game into extra innings. It was an obvious extra reward for Dempster's determination, which began with an off-season training regimen that would leave most athletes gasping.

Left, Ryan Dempster made sure the Cubs weren't holding the bag with his switch to the rotation.
PHIL VELASQUEZ

Still wide-eyed about the game he loves, Dempster blossomed as a starter. **PHIL VELASQUEZ**

"I didn't want to come back and be an average starting pitcher," he said. "I wanted to come back and be a better starting pitcher than I was before. And I knew, mentally I knew, I had the opportunity to do it because of knowledge and experience, but that physically it wasn't going to be easy."

Dempster hadn't pitched 100 innings since 2003, so he knew he would have to climb mountains, literally, to prepare his body for the long haul. He hired a personal trainer, turned his Colorado garage into a gym and went through workouts that included runs at high altitudes, agility drills and weightlifting to strengthen his shoulder.

For those who doubted his passion and dedication

His powerful delivery helped Dempster establish a career high in wins. **CHARLES CHERNEY**

to the serious side of the game, they only had to look at the results.

"Not to brag," Dempster said, "but I felt I worked as hard as anybody in the entire major leagues in the off-season."

He did it all with a passion that belied his public persona of being the ultimate Harry Caray impersonator.

"I would be naïve and stupid if I believed I could just train a little bit and go through my normal off-season workout and then go for 200 innings," Dempster said. "I knew I'd have to work as hard as I've ever worked in my life. I knew if I would do that, I would be a [key] piece to our team."

A key piece? Maybe the key piece, although arguments could be made for almost any Cub. By the All-Star break Dempster was 10-1 at Wrigley Field, and beating Sabathia gave him a career-high 16 wins.

The return to a starting spot had been completed, to the surprise of many preseason skeptics. The doubt

helped push Dempster even harder, as those who predicted failure watched him throw 100 and then 200 innings.

"The longer it goes, the more I'm going to hear it," he said. "That's why I continue to do what I do, like work on the days off. I can't enjoy the success.

"I know people are just waiting for me to mess up, and I understand that. I'd just like to keep doing my thing and starting every fifth day and giving us a chance to win."

He did and he did.

Just before the All-Star break, Dempster said, "I'd like to throw about 250 innings, because that means we're playing into late October."

And that, of course, would help make his prediction come true.

"I got a taste of the postseason [last fall] for the first time in my career," he said, "and I know now I want a chance to start a game in the postseason."

30 TED LILLY

Steve Rosenbloom sits down with the determined lefty

WE'RE AWARE of where we are, but the best thing about it is guys on the club aren't satisfied. We went to the playoffs last year, had an early exit, and that wasn't a good feeling. We want to make sure that that doesn't happen again.

IT'S POSSIBLE last year that we tried to do too much. Speaking for myself, I can certainly say that was what happened in my case — trying to be someone I wasn't, trying to throw harder than I did. And maybe some of the rest of the guys tried to do that in facets of their game, whether it was hitting, fielding or whatever. Maybe have a little more focus, but don't try to do so much that it takes you out of your game.

Squeezing everything he can out of his motion, Lilly fires with Cincinnati's Jeff Keppinger on base in the Cubs' 2-1 loss Aug. 20. **PHIL VELASQUEZ**

fortunate to be on some very, very talented staffs in my career. But this is special for its own reasons.

THE BEST PITCHING LESSON I learned is probably that at no point can you become satisfied with where you are. There's always ways to get better, whether physically or mentally. I think there was a point when I was in Toronto where I felt, "I've kind of got it, and I'm going to repeat this and I'm going to show up and win games." That was in '04 or something. I knew that I didn't know it all, but I did think that I had it pegged a little bit, that I could do my work, go through the motions, show up and win. I went out in '05 and couldn't get anybody out. That was a reality check. This game is just not that easy.

I THINK LOU believes that pitching is a very distinct advantage from one club to the next, depending on the pitching staff. Without it, regardless of what type of offense you have, it's very tough to win.

I THINK PITCHING is a huge part of momentum too. If we can hold the opposition to minimal runs and the offense can find ways to scrap out runs, especially here in the National League, you can win that way. It's been proven over the years.

MY GREAT-GRANDFATHER was working for Teddy Roosevelt and named my grandfather Theodore Roosevelt Lilly. My grandfather named my dad Theodore Roosevelt Jr. He passed it on to me.

WHEN I WAS A KID, football was my favorite sport. That's what I wanted to do. I'd have loved to have Samardzija's opportunity (3). He loves baseball more. I think it's more of a passion for him than football.

I'M GOING TO BE HONEST with you: When I'm out there, I feel like Carlos (1) is acting. But I try not to do that because if I start getting carried away, it's so hard for me to get back and make pitches. Carlos has done that for a while. He's used to that.

I'LL TELL YOU when I would get excited: If I was a closer and the game was over and we won. Then I'd get excited. But it's really hard to get excited when you get out of a jam in the fourth inning and we're winning 1-0. It's the fourth inning. I still have a lot of work to do.

I THINK the one here (2), the first thing I think of is consistency. At least as much as any other. I've been

I THINK LAST YEAR our expectations were to get to the playoffs first and then go from there. This year just getting to the playoffs isn't going to be sufficient. You know what? For myself, for a lot of guys, I don't think we'd go home content unless we win the last game of the postseason. I mean, really.

1 — Teammate Carlos Zambrano. 2 — The Cubs' pitching staff. 3 — To come out of college with pro prospects in football and baseball.

38
CARLOS ZAMBRANO

Emotions on the sleeve that covers an elite arm   By **PAUL SULLIVAN**

When he's on the mound, Zambrano is power personified. **NUCCIO DINUZZO**

HE CUT BACK on his Red Bull intake, his coffee consumption and his on-field temper tantrums.

He increased his potassium by eating more bananas, punched a hole in a wall near his locker, spit out part of a tooth on the mound, led the league in water-cooler tossing, became the first pitcher in 88 years to deliver an RBI in eight straight starts and threw the first no-hitter of his career.

His nickname is Big Z, and, truth be told, Carlos Zambrano might be the most interesting man in the baseball world.

Zambrano did it all this year. It started the first day of spring training, when he hazed new teammate Kosuke Fukudome by wearing the outfielder's No. 1 jersey and reminding the Japanese star that "Carlos Zambrano is the real No. 1."

Zambrano settled comfortably into the spotlight early in his Cubs career, assuming the role of edgy ace with a great sinking fastball and a Hollywood flair for dramatics. He cashed in on his talent and popularity in August 2007, signing a $91.5 million contract extension that made him baseball's second-highest-paid pitcher.

The pressure of living up to that contract was something Zambrano knew he had to face head on in 2008, and mostly he was up to the task. But a stint on the disabled list for shoulder soreness and another 12-day rest in September brought on by recurring shoulder issues and Hurricane Ike-induced postponements prevented Zambrano from having one of his typically dominant seasons.

His earned-run average was up and his strikeout total was down, but Zambrano remained one of the most difficult pitchers to hit in the National League. He ranked among the league leaders in winning percentage as well.

The yin and yang of his season came into focus in the final two months. After going 1-1 with a 7.11 ERA from Aug. 9 through Sept. 2, Zambrano turned in the game of his life Sept. 14 at Miller Park when he no-hit Houston on 11 days' rest.

"I guess I'm back," he said with a smile.

While Zambrano flashed stretches of undeniable greatness, he also endured a couple of ugly slumps, shoulder and neck issues and the age-old problem of cramping in his forearm. He took himself out of one game after five innings and said afterward he had been "mentally prepared" to go only five or six. His mood swings got the best of him on several occasions, including dugout outbursts in Washington, Pittsburgh and Los Angeles. He attacked a couple of water coolers after giving up seven runs and a career-high 13 hits to the Dodgers.

Manager Lou Piniella tried to get his excitable ace to calm down and stop showing his frustration when things went wrong.

"I told him to stop expending all that energy fighting himself," Piniella said. "Relax. Concentrate on the hitter and get people out. Why fight himself, let the other team know he's frustrated? It's defeating the purpose all the way around."

But after a while, even Piniella gave up.

Zambrano was never going to change, and the good stretches of pitching were worth putting up with the petulant moments and penchant for throwing things or punching walls. Perhaps it was a sign of maturity that he did not punch a teammate, as he had done in '07.

Emotion is what fuels Zambrano and makes him the pitcher he knows he can be, the one who no-hit the Astros and allowed only two balls out of the infield. Showing a little emotion at work is as natural as breathing for Big Z.

"Always," he said. "You're talking with Carlos Zambrano, man. Always."

Zambrano takes his hitting almost as seriously as his pitching. **PHIL VELASQUEZ**

The glare of Notre Dame helped Samardzija adjust to the majors quickly. **PHIL VELASQUEZ**

29
JEFF SAMARDZIJA

Steve Rosenbloom traces the pitcher's path from Notre Dame to Wrigley

I REPORTED to spring training and pitched well there, so they wanted to make me a starter. So I went down to minor-league camp. Started at Double A, pitched pretty well. Went to Triple A, pitched pretty well. Got called up here and been in the pen ever since. It's been a pretty crazy year.

I'M USED to having 35 minutes to warm up. Changing that to five minutes is a little different.

WE WERE ALL the way out in Tucson, and there weren't any amazing flight times out of Tucson to Chicago, so I had to go from Tucson to Vegas to Chicago. I was up all night, didn't get any sleep, got here about 7, showed up at the park about 9 for a day game, worked out and threw two innings that day. So that was pretty wild.

GOING OUT THERE and striking out the first guy was pretty crazy.

IT CAME DOWN to the situation (1). The Cubbies had drafted me, I'm kind of a local kid (2), I'd been watching them for a long time. And on top of that, it was baseball. It was what I loved to do and what I enjoy doing every day.

I WENT AND PLAYED the Blue-Gold game in the morning, caught a touchdown. Fun day. The next day I came out and pitched seven innings and got the win against a Big East team.

I THINK THEY'D GET ALONG (3). They're both demanding. They respect the players who play the game right and do it for the right reasons. If you go out and play the game hard, they're going to like you and give you your shot. That's all you can ask for.

THEY'RE A LOT ALIKE (4). Both are really old, for

Samardzija slaps hands with Mike Fontenot, Derrek Lee and Mark DeRosa.
PHIL VELASQUEZ

one. There's a little mystique-slash-inconvenience that goes along with that. You kind of adapt to it. I remember at Notre Dame before they changed a lot of it, there were wire lockers and stuff like that.

MY DAD WAS a work-at-the-mills kind of guy. My mom was a secretary at the elementary school. My mom was the cushion, my dad was the hammer. My dad expected a lot out of us. That's why when people ask about Lou and Charlie, I just kind of laugh because if I made it through my childhood years with my pops, then anything else is a cake-walk.

I'M AN AMAZING Ping Pong player. I'll be very cocky about that.

1 — Deciding between baseball and football. 2 — From Merrillville, Ind. 3 — Notre Dame coach Charlie Weis and Cubs manager Lou Piniella. 4 — Notre Dame Stadium and Wrigley Field. 5 — The World Series.

Working with absolutey filthy stuff, Marmol earned an All-Star bid this year. **CHARLES CHERNEY**
Right, Marmol laughs it up with teammates in Arizona. **PHIL VELASQUEZ**

49
CARLOS MARMOL

Top-notch reliever rides out troubles, then rebounds   By **FRED MITCHELL**

CARLOS MARMOL considers himself a student of the game, and his most influential teacher has been veteran teammate Kerry Wood.

As the Cubs' ace setup man and occasional closer, the 25-year-old Marmol endured a rare period of ineffectiveness midway through the 2008 season. That's when Wood's sage counsel really began to pay dividends.

"I've given him advice," Wood said. "He's very curious, and he wants to do the right things and [learn] how to act and how to pitch to certain people in certain situations.

"He's my throwing partner every day. We talk about pitching quite a bit. Whether it has helped or not, who knows? But he has been eager to learn, and he asks a lot of questions."

Marmol was added to the major-league roster in November 2005. The right-hander with the devastating slider achieved almost immediate success at the big-league level. In 2007 he finished with a 5-1 record and a 1.43 earned-run average in 59 appearances.

"He has been very good for us," rookie catcher Geovany Soto said. "Early in the year he was lights out. He did fall into a little funk. Every pitcher goes through it. After the All-Star break, he got it back together. He has been huge. I don't think we would have been here without Marmol."

It was during his struggles that Marmol sought Wood's advice.

"It's important to talk to Kerry because we help each other," said Marmol, a native of the Dominican Republic. "I learn from him. We learn from the mistakes we make, and we talk a lot. I'm glad he is helping me."

Marmol returned to his normal confident self on the mound as the end of the regular season approached, and his numbers responded.

"Kerry Wood has taken Marmol under his wing to prepare him for the bullpen role," Soto said. "Woody has been trying to get him going as a setup guy or closer. He has been huge for Marmol, and Marmol has been picking up a lot of stuff from Woody and the other guys."

Marquis converses with catcher Geovany Soto before the right-hander's first start April 5 against Houston. The Cubs won 9-7. **BONNIE TRAFELET**

21 JASON MARQUIS

Steve Rosenbloom hears the righty explain the mental side

I'VE BEEN IN SITUATIONS — for example, the 2006 Cardinals — where we weren't the best team in the playoffs, but we won the World Series. We got hot at the right time.

THEN AGAIN, on the 2004 World Series team with the Cardinals, I thought we had the best team in baseball, and we got beat.

WE HAVE A QUIET confidence. We're not running

around saying, "We're the best team in baseball. We're going to win this thing." We know we have a very good chance, and we believe in ourselves.

I ALWAYS SAID it can't be physical (1) if I feel as good now as I did at the end of '04 and '05 and '06 and '07. So I started working with a sports psychologist. I really felt like I was so much looking at the big picture and what kind of season I could have, looking too far down the road and worrying about my final

Often a beast as a hitter, Marquis breaks his bat this time. **NUCCIO DINUZZO**

the game, and obviously he's been blessed with great teams and not-so-great teams, and he's found a way.

OVER HERE WITH LOU, you know what you're going to get. He wears his emotions on his sleeve. He's more of a reactive guy. I feel like he's a guy who whether he's trying to teach you a lesson or yell at you, he's doing it for your own good and there's nothing personal about it. That's just Lou's personality. Some players can handle it, some can't.

YOU HAVE TO GIVE Greg Maddux credit. Tom Glavine. John Smoltz. Guys who have modernized the way of pitching and taken it to new levels. To be fortunate enough to play with three guys of that magnitude on the same team really helped me learn what I needed to do, not only to be a big-league pitcher but stay a big-league pitcher.

CHRIS CARPENTER never gave a pitch away, never gave an inning away, no matter what the score was. Every pitch meant something.

IN REALITY, when you look at it, it's a matter of focusing for maybe 500 seconds for that day, if you really break it down. You're throwing 110 pitches, so you really have to focus for the three or four seconds that you step on the rubber before you release the ball. You break it down and simplify it that way, and I think a lot more guys would succeed.

THAT'S ONE OF THE REASONS I signed with the Cubs — the fans. Coming in with the Cardinals and the great rivalry we have with them, to see the fans so passionate about the game and into the game, and also feel for them being so frustrated for so many years and still coming out and still having that hope that we can win is fun to see. I wanted to be a part of a team that could bring a championship to the city. I grew up in New York, so I have an idea of what type of mayhem it would be. But words won't describe and pictures won't describe what would go on in the city if that was to come about. We're trying our butts off, and we believe we have a good enough team to do it.

stats and not worrying about the little things that will get you those big final numbers and get to getting the ball in the postseason. I was able to take a step back and look more at the smaller things of pitch by pitch, inning by inning that will add up to throwing the ball well. I take each day as its own.

I WISH I could take the ball and start every day.

BOBBY (2) IS MORE of a laid-back, out-of-the-scenes type of guy, especially in the clubhouse. He lets you do your work and leaves you alone. Obviously, he gets fired up in the course of a game if a call doesn't go the team's way.

THEN I GET TRADED over to St. Louis. Tony (3) is a very intelligent baseball guy. He crosses every T, dots every I, makes sure everything is in place from stats on hitters to stats on pitchers. He's a real student of

1 — His recurring slumps in the second halves of seasons. 2 — Braves manager Bobby Cox. 3 — Cardinals manager Tony La Russa.

Following page
The 11-4 victory Aug. 6 over the Astros explains the sea of "W" flags in the bleachers. **PHIL VELASQUEZ**

25 DERREK LEE

Low-key first baseman can deliver high-powered offense

By **FRED MITCHELL**

WHEN DERREK LEE is performing at his optimum, the game seems to come easily for him.

With grace, strength and coordination, he rifles line drives all over the ballpark. In the field, hard-hit balls seem drawn to his first baseman's glove like metal to a magnet. Throws in the dirt from other infielders? No problem: D-Lee has the scoop.

In that sense, Lee's low-key personality and laid-back approach to the game seem to mesh.

"I don't go out seeking attention," the Cubs' rock-steady 33-year-old first baseman said. "When it comes, I just deal with it."

Lee is a two-time All-Star and a three-time Gold Glove winner. His father, Leon, a longtime star in Japanese professional baseball, served as the Cubs' Pacific Rim scouting coordinator from 1998-2002.

Lee has demonstrated such robotic consistency over his career that his occasional struggles at the plate are cause for concern. His best season was 2005, when he hit a league-best .335, walloped 46 home runs and drove in 107 runs. He also led the NL with 50 doubles.

He set a lofty standard for himself, one that is nearly impossible to duplicate on a yearly basis.

"I think the numbers depend on your teammates," Lee said. "You can't drive yourself in all the time. You've got to have guys on base. We have a great lineup, and with the guys in front of me, there are going to be guys on base."

Lee has been remarkably durable, but a fractured wrist limited him to 50 games in 2006. He rebounded with an All-Star season in 2007, hitting .317 with 22 home runs and 43 doubles in 150 games. He won his third Gold Glove, and he was awarded the MLB Players Association Heart and Hustle Award for the Cubs because of his charitable endeavors.

Milwaukee Brewers broadcaster Davey Nelson, a former big-league infielder and first-base coach, said he used to shake hands with Lee at the start of every game.

"But I told him I don't want him to touch me because he's so hot he might burn my hand," Nelson said.

Lee slaps hands with infield mate Aramis Ramirez after the third baseman's homer in an April victory. **NUCCIO DINUZZO**

Lee, however, bemoaned the fact that "I never got hot" during the 2008 season as the No. 3 hitter in Lou Piniella's lineup. Still, he put up very respectable numbers and insisted that his previously injured wrist and a sore neck that bothered him in August were not responsible for his diminished home run total.

"My goals are always team-oriented, so that's really

The lanky, powerful Lee uncoils on a solo home run off Ben Sheets in a 10-7 loss to the Brewers on April 29.
NUCCIO DINUZZO

all that concerns me," Lee said.

To be sure, the 2008 Cubs accomplished their regular-season goal by winning the NL Central Division. With Lee's bat showing signs of life as the regular season wound down, they set their sights on winning a World Series.

Lee, a 6-foot-5-inch, 245-pound native of Sacramento, turned down numerous college scholarship offers to sign with San Diego after the Padres picked him in the first round of the 1993 amateur draft. He was traded to

Florida in 1998 and played for the Marlins' 2003 World Series winners. The Cubs acquired him from Florida before the 2004 season. He is signed through 2010.

In 2006, Lee created a foundation to fight Leber's congenital amaurosis, a degenerative eye disease that results in loss of vision. The effort, titled "Project 3000," includes fundraising efforts to provide state-of-the-art genetic testing for everyone in the U.S. Lee's young daughter, Jada Ryan, has been diagnosed with the disease.

DeRosa pops up from his slide as he scores in a 4-3 loss to the Padres on May 13. **NUCCIO DINUZZO**

7 MARK DeROSA

Solid, versatile and well-spoken, he's a pro's pro By **DAN McGRATH**

THE BASEBALL AXIOM about some of the best trades being the ones that aren't made was certainly true for the Cubs this season.

Throughout spring training, rumors were strong that the Cubs were discussing a deal involving Brian Roberts, Baltimore's outstanding second baseman and leadoff hitter. But they were unable to pull the trigger, and that failure wound up benefiting the Cubs.

Roberts, safe to say, would have been a good player in Chicago. But his arrival would have meant diminished time for someone who emerged as one of the Cubs' best and most consistent players, the versatile Mark DeRosa.

"He's certainly had a nice year for us," manager Lou Piniella said. "He's a solid major-league ballplayer who always gives you a big-league effort."

Indeed, DeRosa established career highs in hits, walks, home runs, RBIs, on-base percentage and slugging percentage. He homered in four straight games during one mid-August stretch and was effective no matter where he hit in the order or played in the field.

The 33-year-old veteran was the Cubs' second baseman of record, but he filled in seamlessly when deployed in right field or left field, at third base or even shortstop. Playing right field, he helped preserve Carlos Zambrano's no-hitter with a running catch of Geoff Blum's liner toward the corner leading off the eighth inning against Houston on Sept. 14 in Milwaukee.

"The thing about DeRo is he's such a good athlete that no matter where you put him, he looks like he belongs," observed Cubs TV analyst Bob Brenly, a multiple-position guy in his playing days. "A lot of guys — most guys — change positions, and they're out of their comfort zone. With DeRo, you can use him at four or five spots and not miss a beat. He's going to play the position."

DeRosa's athletic ability was on display as early as his high school days. He was all-state in football and baseball at Bergen Catholic High School in Oradell, N.J. He excelled in both sports at the college level as well, starting at quarterback for the University of Pennsylvania from 1993-95 and leading the Quakers to two Ivy League titles.

The Atlanta Braves picked him in the seventh round of the 1996 amateur draft, but unlike Cubs teammate and fellow two-sport star Jeff Samardzija, DeRosa wasn't confronted with a baseball-football dilemma regarding his professional future.

"The NFL doesn't have much interest in 6-1, 200-pound guys with no mobility," he said.

His self-deprecating humor and engaging personality made DeRosa one of the most popular Cubs. He writes a blog for the team's Web site and offers thoughtful insights and analysis in postgame media sessions.

But he's all business between the lines, having learned the game as a valuable utility man on Braves playoff teams in 2001-04, then signing with the Cubs as a free agent after two years with Texas.

And though he's not a stats guy, DeRosa was thrilled to reach 20 home runs and 80 RBIs for the first time in his career in 2008. Piniella promised he'd be excused from some of next spring's more onerous bus trips if he achieved those milestones.

"I'm done with Tucson," DeRosa said with a smile.

"I don't worry about personal stuff," he added. "I've done well this year. You always want to do better. ... Maybe in the off-season you can say, 'OK, that was a good year, and here's what I have to improve on next year.'"

The Cubs would be more than happy with a replay. Brian who?

Following page
Longtime teammates Fontenot and Theriot trot off the field together. **BONNIE TRAFELET**

17 MIKE FONTENOT

The infielders' shared history ranges ...

2 RYAN THERIOT

... From high school to Wrigley Field By **MELISSA ISAACSON**

Theriot fires to first base over the slide of Juan Pierre to complete a double play against the Dodgers on May 28.
NUCCIO DINUZZO

RYAN THERIOT and Mike Fontenot have more in common than their Louisiana roots, a love of Cajun food and baby-faced looks that prompted Alfonso Soriano to mistake Fontenot for a batboy last year.

Being handpicked by a manager who knows what he likes is something both players can appreciate.

"I love the kid," Lou Piniella said of Theriot, the Cubs' third-round pick in 2001, after easing him in at shortstop last season in place of Cesar Izturis and ahead of Ronny Cedeno. "He plays hard, has energy,

plays to win, is confident — all the qualities you like in a baseball player.

"Nobody gave him anything. He's earned everything. He took the job over. He forced me to write his name in the lineup."

A similar case could be made for Fontenot, a first-round pick by Baltimore in 2001 who worked his way through the minor leagues and reached the majors with the Cubs in '05 after being included in the Sammy Sosa trade.

Fontenot jokes that one day he'll tell his grandchildren he was traded for Sosa. He can also tell them he's the only one involved in the deal who's still with the Cubs, something he came to appreciate when he finally stuck in 2007.

"I didn't know exactly what to expect coming in," Fontenot said. "I knew they probably would have an open spot on the infield, so I took the approach to move around, keep working on things."

For Theriot, the 2008 season has been a breakout year in which he firmly established himself as the everyday shortstop. Beyond that, he maintained a .300-plus batting average and was among the league leaders in hits and multiple-hit games.

"He's a good player," Piniella said. "He's got some speed. He listens. He works hard, and he's a winning player. Shortstop is a tough position to play. But he's done a heck of a job.

"He's a confident kid. If there's one thing a young major-league player needs, it's confidence, and he's got plenty of it."

Theriot came out of the gate red-hot, batting .340 in April and reaching the All-Star break at .320. Though he wore down a bit in early September, no one was doubting Theriot would continue to provide the intangibles that have become his trademark.

"I'm going to play hard, give it everything I've got," he said. "And I'm not afraid to fail. I'll do whatever it takes to help the team win. I take pride in my defense. Either you drive them in or you've got to save a run."

Fontenot is nicknamed Chicken because of a chicken-like dance he once did in the minors, he says. He shares Theriot's work ethic, but because he is generously listed at 5 feet 8 inches, Fontenot was often underestimated, particularly for his power at the plate.

After being called up from Triple-A Iowa in June 2007 for the second time in less than a month, Fontenot went on a tear. He hit safely in 17 of 18 games, including a 10-game hitting streak and a towering home run that cleared Wrigley Field's right-field bleachers and reached Sheffield Avenue.

Continuing his super-sub role in '08, Fontenot found his stroke in July, hitting .365 (19-for-52) with six doubles, a triple and four home runs. He was productive in August as well, batting .314, and flirted with .300 for the season.

In the field, Fontenot flourished alongside Theriot. That is hardly surprising. The two were youth baseball and high school contemporaries who finally teamed up at LSU. Yet both say their relationship has never been a rivalry.

"Ever since I've known him, we've been good friends, helping each other out, rooting for each other," Fontenot said.

Theriot, drafted lower but a big-leaguer sooner, agreed.

"We've been like brothers for a long time," he said.

When Fontenot was called up in '07, the two shared a laugh when Cubs coach Alan Trammell suggested they work on double plays and attempt to "get used to each other." Not only were they the double-play combination that led LSU to the College World Series title in 2000, they figured that counting high school all-star games, college ball and Triple-A Iowa, they had probably played shortstop and second base together "400, 500, 600 games," Theriot said.

The two also share food tastes and family values, and "a lot of our hobbies are the same," Fontenot said. "We like to hunt and fish. Our families are friends. He just wants to contribute, and I'm like that too. Wherever it is, just put me in and I'll play."

Even after a breakout season, Theriot is not satisfied.

"I always want to feel like I have something to prove," he said. "I always go out there thinking there's somebody right behind me who is more capable than me. I know there are people in the minor leagues who are going 'I can do what he does,' because I did it. To say, 'I've made it, that's it, I'm a major-league shortstop,' that's all fine and dandy, but it can be gone in a day."

16 ARAMIS RAMIREZ

Steve Rosenbloom listens to the 3rd baseman's story

I'M HAPPY with my season because every year I pretty much do the same thing: hit for a decent average, hit a decent number of homers and drive in 100 or more. But I'm happier this year because of the way we're playing.

IN THE PLAYOFFS, pitching is going to get you beat. It's not the offense.

WHEN SAMMY WAS HERE and Moises in '05 and '04 and '03, we had great lineups, but we didn't have as good pitching as we have this year. We have great starting pitching and a great bullpen. Woody in the bullpen with Marmol and Samardzija, and getting Harden from Oakland and getting Z healthy ... this is the best pitching we've had in a long time here.

I DON'T PAY ATTENTION to what they say about the Gold Glove because I can't control that. I just go out there and try to do my job.

I WAS 24, 25 when I got traded here. I was only going to get better. I worked on it a lot. I used to make a lot of young mistakes. Everybody goes through it. You mature as a player.

WE HAVE A LOT of poor people (1). But there's a lot of rich people and a lot of middle-class people. I wasn't poor. I was decent. My dad is a doctor and my mother is an accountant, so I had a decent life.

I MISSED ONE YEAR of baseball because my dad wanted me to finish high school. He wouldn't let me sign. I was 15 when I was going to sign my first con-tract, but he didn't let me sign because he wanted me to finish school.

I WAS GETTING good grades. I had to. I had no choice.

I USED TO WATCH a lot of Toronto games when I was 13, 14. I used to like George Bell. He was a good hitter, and everybody in the Dominican followed him. He was like the only power hitter we had in the majors back then. He was an MVP in Toronto and led the league in homers and had 130 ribbies. He was good.

I KNOW HE PLAYED here, but that was at the end, and he wasn't that good then.

IT'S AMAZING what kind of fans this city can bring. They're something else. Everywhere we go, we feel like we're at home. Every hotel. Every city.

I DIDN'T KNOW we were going to go to Milwaukee (2) until 10 on Saturday night, and I showed up the next day in Milwaukee, and there were 23,000 fans there with one-day notice. That's pretty good. It was raining. It was ugly out there. And they still drove to Milwaukee to watch us play. It's amazing.

ACTUALLY, I MET the guy I really wanted to meet when I was young. I met Michael Jordan here in Chicago. That's really the only guy I wanted to shake his hand. That might be the only guy I wanted to take a picture with, and I did.

DON'T TAKE ANYTHING for granted. When you think you've got everything, when you think you have your best season, everything can go away in a week. You can be feeling good and hitting good and playing good defense, and one day to another, everything can change. So don't take anything for granted.

The sight of Ramirez rounding the bases has become familiar at Wrigley Field. **JOSE M. OSORIO**

Following page
The field, the ivy, the fans, the sky ... need you ask more about Wrigley Field? **PHIL VELASQUEZ**

1 — In his hometown of Santo Domingo, Dominican Republic. 2 — To play Houston in the series displaced by Hurricane Ike.

12 ALFONSO SORIANO

Playoffs the perfect time for outfielder to step up By **PHIL ROGERS**

EARTH TO Alfonso Soriano, come in please. Earth to Soriano … Earth to Soriano … report in, please.

That was the first paragraph in a game story after a Cubs loss in Pittsburgh in May. At the airport later that night, a gate agent got on the microphone and started asking baseball trivia questions, trying to entertain a bored group of fans awaiting a flight home.

One interrupted to provide his own question. "Who is the worst left fielder in the National League?" he asked, and the group exploded in laughter.

This didn't seem much of a reach at the time, as mistakes by Soriano in the field and on the bases had contributed to the Cubs losing one game in 14 innings and another in 11.

"Tough loss," manager Lou Piniella said. "Let's just regroup at home, forget about what happened and go about our business. That's all I have to say about the last two days. Too many mistakes."

Throughout the 2008 season, the exciting Soriano was both an All-Star and an accident waiting to happen. But as September ended he was a leadoff hitter on a division champion, just as he had been in 2007.

With his legs appearing vulnerable to muscle pulls and strains since he came to Chicago, Soriano has rarely been the speed-power package he had been earlier in his career. But his signing with the Cubs two winters ago for an eight-year, $136 million bonanza that is the biggest in club history still appears to have been a turning point that awakened a sleeping giant of a franchise.

Before Soriano arrived, the Cubs had made the playoffs four times since World War II, most recently in 2003. With Soriano providing a presence at the top of the order, the Cubs are headed into October for the second year in a row.

It will be the fifth time in Soriano's eight full big-

Soriano has developed a trademark hop as he catches fly balls. **PHIL VELASQUEZ**

Left, it's high-fives all around after another Soriano home run.
PHIL VELASQUEZ

league seasons that his teams have rolled into October, the exceptions coming during his two seasons in Texas and one in Washington after he was traded for Alex Rodriguez.

Think about that: Traded for Alex Rodriguez. Not a bad line on the resume.

But Soriano has his critics, and always has.

"If he's a foundation piece, why has he changed teams so much?" a Major League Baseball executive asked after Soriano signed with the Cubs. "He's a .280 lifetime hitter and a liability in the field. I don't understand it myself."

Since Soriano arrived in Chicago, critics have carped that his desire to swing for the fences and infrequent walks make him a better candidate to hit fifth or sixth than first. But a surprisingly patient Piniella prefers Soriano in the leadoff spot and isn't known to have ever seriously considered dropping him in the order.

Soriano has been sidelined by injuries three times in his two seasons with the Cubs, including two stints in 2008. He was on the disabled list with a strained quadriceps muscle in April and then was out 33 games after breaking a wrist when Atlanta's Jeff Bennett hit him with a pitch.

The Cubs played well during Soriano's first absence, going 9-5, but were only 16-17 when he was out with the broken wrist. Piniella couldn't wait to get him back, and Soriano immediately rewarded him with a run-scoring double.

Leadoff home runs have been a staple of Soriano's two seasons in Chicago. The Cubs would love to see some of them in October, but he hasn't delivered with regularity in postseason games, going 2-for-14 in the Cubs' three losses to Arizona last year.

Earth to Soriano … earth to Soriano … it's time to quiet the critics.

15 JIM EDMONDS

Former enemy becomes a darling in center field   By **PAUL SULLIVAN**

IT WASN'T EXACTLY the kind of welcome Jim Edmonds had hoped for when he made his Cubs debut on a beautiful spring afternoon at Wrigley Field.

The Cubs had signed the outfielder after San Diego released him. In light of Felix Pie's disappointing start, it was a low-risk, high-reward move by general manager Jim Hendry.

But the memories of Edmonds' antics at Wrigley while wearing a Cardinals uniform were fresh in the minds of grudge-holding Cubs fans, who viewed him with skepticism when he arrived in Chicago.

Carlos Zambrano issued a brusque "no comment" when asked about his new teammate. Edmonds had shown up Zambrano with a spin-o-rama move at the plate after hitting a home run onto Sheffield Avenue during a game in 2004. Zambrano yelled at Edmonds as he rounded the bases, and the pitcher never forgot the slight.

But the former rivals hugged when Edmonds arrived May 15, and he received a standing ovation when he stepped in against the Padres' Greg Maddux in the second inning of his debut. Edmonds went 1-for-4, but he was booed in the seventh after striking out with the bases loaded.

Male-sensitivity expert Phil Donahue, who was at Wrigley to sing during the seventh-inning stretch, was shocked by Cubs fans' reaction to the new acquisition.

"He strikes out, he walks back to the dugout and they're booing him," Donahue told the Tribune. "He's got to be saying, 'I thought this was the Friendly Confines.' But you pay your ticket price, and this is what you get to do. Only in America."

Edmonds said he didn't mind the booing, as he'd certainly never been cheered at Wrigley.

"And I've been booed louder," he said. "It's baseball at its best. I'd rather have that than a bunch of people just sitting there being quiet. It's what I like to hear when I'm out there."

Edmonds struggled out of the gate with the Cubs, starting 4-for-24, and by late May it looked as if the experiment would be brief. But after being booed for committing an error May 30 against Colorado,

The new Cub in town loosens up before his first game May 15, a 4–0 win over the Padres. **PHIL VELASQUEZ**

Defensive gems like this, on which Edmonds robbed Cincinnati's Jerry Hairston Jr., have become commonplace.
SCOTT STRAZZANTE

he went 3-for-4 with a homer and four RBIs in a comeback victory. Edmonds said he hoped fans would come to his side "sooner or later."

"Sometimes when I'm in the outfield, I think I'm still wearing red and white," he said with a smile.

That game was Edmonds' turnaround. He practically carried the team in June, hitting .319 with six home runs and 19 RBIs. The tide had turned, and when his ex-manager, Tony La Russa, criticized Edmonds for disavowing his Cardinals past, the resulting war of words finally seemed to earn Edmonds his Cubs stripes.

Edmonds cooled down a bit in the second half and lost some playing time in September but was always capable of a clutch hit or a great catch, like the one Sept. 15 against Houston in Milwaukee that kept Ted Lilly's no-hit bid intact the day after Zambrano's no-hitter.

"Jim is amazing," Lilly said. "His instincts are as good or better than anyone I've ever seen in the outfield. He pays attention to what the pitcher is trying to do and the kind of swings the hitter is taking. He's just got a great feel for the game."

It took a while before Cubs fans got a real feel for Edmonds.

But once they looked beyond his red-clad past and watched him play, they finally realized a vintage Edmonds in Cubs pinstripes would do just fine.

9 REED JOHNSON

Nothing stops scrappy outfielder, including walls   By **DAVE VAN DYCK**

IT WILL BE REPLAYED as long as there are highlight shows and rehashed as long as people have a reason to remember the Cubs' 2008 season.

It is the catch, Reed Johnson's unrehearsed dive into stardom and the hearts of Cubs fans everywhere, the bill of his cap turned upward from his encounter with the wall April 25 in Washington.

"At Wrigley Field they might have had to call a time-out to find his head in the vines," manager Lou Piniella said.

Johnson also was able to laugh about it later, but sliding headfirst into a concrete wall can be a scary thing.

"Being early in the season, it was good to kind of send that message that this guy will run through walls to try to make a play," Johnson said.

People like Piniella took notice, and it helped Johnson get more playing time, which didn't figure to be easy for a guy who joined the team after being released by Toronto.

Johnson's aggressive, all-out style and unbridled enthusiasm in the clubhouse made him a sparkplug on a team that was somewhat laid back.

"I don't know if I would think of it in those words, but I just try to play hard every day," Johnson said. "My goal is to make a defensive play or try to get a rally started by leading off with a hit, walk, hit by pitch, bunt, any way to get on to help the team score a run.

"And if that's what people consider a sparkplug, that's an honor."

Johnson is one of baseball's lucky players, actually joining a better team and getting more playing time after being released.

"It's been a blessing for me to come to [the Cubs]," he said. "There's just no other place I'd rather be. Hopefully I've played well enough this year to stick around for a while. That's a big part of my goal here, too, not only to win a World Series but to be able to come back and help this team win again in the future."

To show Johnson's value to the Cubs, he batted over .350 with runners on base. He also reached double figures in getting hit by pitches.

"I'm not trying to get hit," he said. "I'm going to take my approach up to the plate, look for a ball and try to drive it the other way. If a pitcher comes hard in on me — that is what a lot of teams like to do — and I'm standing on the plate, sometimes they miss."

Whatever it takes, just like sliding into an outfield wall headfirst.

But as the Cubs were clinching the Central Division, Johnson was thinking about how close he had become to his teammates, how it was easy for him to bond after being discarded in Toronto.

"That's what we've talked about in here," Johnson said. "We haven't won in 100 years, and it's going to be 25 guys bonded for the rest of their lives. It will be continued until we die, coming back for parades and Opening Days.

"That's what I think is so special about this team, that guys really enjoy being around each other. And hopefully we'll be around each other for a long, long time."

All hustle and heart, Johnson has been a superb addition this season. **PHIL VELASQUEZ**

Fukudome's offense has been inconsistent, but his defense has been stellar. **PHIL VELASQUEZ**

1 KOSUKE FUKUDOME

Fast start gets Japanese outfielder on the map By **DAN McGRATH**

EVEN BEFORE he had played a game for the Cubs, Kosuke Fukudome had ignited fan excitement to a level not seen around Wrigley Field since the slugging heyday of Sammy Sosa, or maybe since the "Sha-won-o-meter" tracked Shawon Dunston's progress as America's fastest-rising young shortstop.

Headbands, T-shirts, posters and all manner of material saluting the Japanese player was out in force on Opening Day at Wrigley, and there was a serious run on all of it after Fukudome swatted a three-run ninth-inning home run off Eric Gagne to pull the Cubs even with the Milwaukee Brewers.

That the Brewers came back to win in the 10th hardly mattered. A star was born, and he was saluted with rhythmic chants of "Fu-ku-DO-me" every time he came to the plate at Wrigley.

"He's a nice ballplayer; he can do a lot of things," manager Lou Piniella said of the former Japanese Central League batting champion and two-time Olympian, who batted .305 with a .416 on-base percentage over his first two months as a Cub.

Fukudome was more than a Wrigley Field phenomenon. He was voted onto the starting lineup of the National League All-Star team with one of the highest totals in fan voting, becoming the first Cubs outfielder to start an All-Star Game since Sosa in 2004.

"My teammates have made the transition pretty easy," Fukudome said.

Alas, National League pitching seemed to catch up with him after the break, as his average dipped into the .260s. But his batting eye was one of the best on the team, as he was among the top Cubs in walks and reached double figures in stolen bases.

More importantly, he remained a valuable contributor by virtue of his stellar play in right field. He made several outstanding catches, including a game-saver when he crashed into the right-field wall to take at least a double away from the Cardinals' Felipe Lopez with two runners on in the eighth inning Sept. 11 at St. Louis. The resulting 3-2 victory helped pull the Cubs out of their only real rough patch of the year, as they had lost eight of their previous 10 games.

Fukudome created an immediate media stir when he arrived in the United States. **PHIL VELASQUEZ**

With the Cubs en route to the playoffs for the second straight season, Fukudome was Chicago's most popular Japanese import since Toyota.

AT WRIGLEY FIELD

Photo essay By **CHRIS WALKER**

Cubs fans wait (somewhat) patiently to enter Wrigley Field for a night game against the Brewers on Sept. 17.

AS THE WORLD gets smaller, the baby-blue Cub cult grows. Roaming the stands at Wrigley Field, I met Laurie Hintz, who became a fan in the 1970s when she got cable TV in North Dakota. Adam Knox of California travels for his job. But he bragged he hasn't missed a game in seven years. He catches them on the Internet.

Tadeusz Wejzner and his daughter, Edyta, explained that they first heard the Cubs mentioned in the movie

"Back to the Future" when they rented it in Poland.

I even met Cubs fans from the South Side. The old-timers may grumble over their beer about the yuppies taking over the neighborhood. And sometimes the games do take on a party atmosphere. But any newcomer can become a die-hard with just one trait: patience.

As the playoffs approached, John Schoenfeld, 60, watched a night game from Wrigley's chilly upper deck. "I've been waiting my whole life," he said.

Clockwise: Torsten Anderson, 4, of Ft. Wayne, Ind., wears the ubiquitous Kosuke Fukudome headband. Soon-to-be-marrried Cubs fans John Festa, 31, and Beth Miller, 32, of Chicago make their way up the ramp at Wrigley Field. Adam Knox, 31, of Thousand Oaks, Calif., says he has not missed a Cubs game — whether by TV, radio or the Internet — in seven years. He came to Chicago for the last homestand. Trudie Achaetel, 63, of Chicago calls herself "The Button Lady" and boasts she went into labor with her first child at Wrigley Field some 40 years ago.

Fans without tickets peer through the "knothole" on Sheffield Avenue.

Previous page
Wearing a super-sized glove, Mike Pech, 14, runs for a ball with
fellow ballhawks on Sheffield Avenue during batting practice.

2008 SEASON PLAYER CARDS
CHICAGO CUBS

CUBS

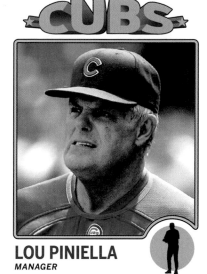

LOU PINIELLA
MANAGER

CUBS

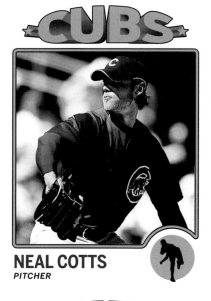

NEAL COTTS
PITCHER

CUBS

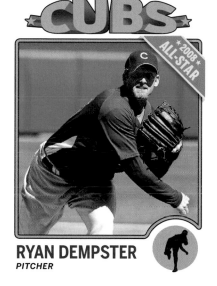

RYAN DEMPSTER
PITCHER

CUBS

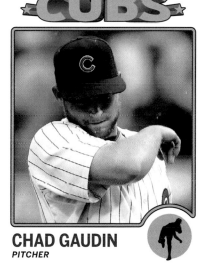

CHAD GAUDIN
PITCHER

CUBS

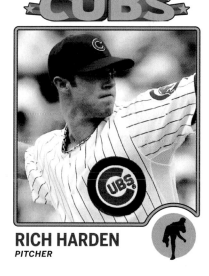

RICH HARDEN
PITCHER

CUBS

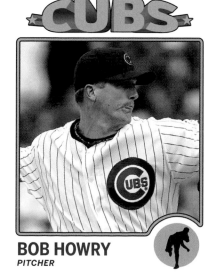

BOB HOWRY
PITCHER

CUBS

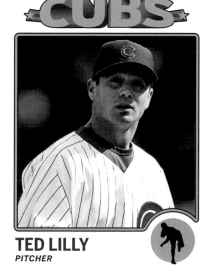

TED LILLY
PITCHER

CUBS

CARLOS MARMOL
PITCHER

NEAL COTTS
NO. 48 ★ PITCHER

HT: 6-1 • WT: 200 • BATS: L • THROWS: L
BORN: 3/25/80 in Lebanon, Ill.
HOW ACQ'D: Trade with White Sox (2006)

CAREER PITCHING STATS

YR.	TEAM	G	IP	H	W	L	SV	BB	SO	ERA
'03	CWS	4	13.1	15	1	1	0	17	10	8.10
'04	CWS	56	65.1	61	4	4	0	30	58	5.65
'05	CWS	69	60.1	38	4	0	0	29	58	1.94
'06	CWS	70	54.0	64	1	2	1	24	43	5.17
'07	CHC	16	16.2	15	0	1	0	9	14	4.86
Totals		**215**	**209.2**	**193**	**10**	**8**	**1**	**109**	**183**	**4.55**

2008 HIGHLIGHTS

★ Posted a streak of 10 straight scoreless appearances, June 18-July 8.

★ Held opponents scoreless in 17 of 23 appearances after July 12.

★ In first 24 appearances on road, ERA was 2.89.

Chicago Tribune Photo by PHIL VELASQUEZ

LOU PINIELLA
NO. 41 ★ MANAGER

BORN: 8/28/43 in Tampa
AS PLAYER: 18 seasons (1964-84) for Orioles, Indians, Royals, Yankees

CAREER MANAGERIAL RECORD

YR.	TEAM	W	L	PCT.	FINISH (GB)	PLAYOFFS
'86	NYY	90	72	.556	2nd (5.5)	—
'87	NYY	89	73	.549	4th (9)	—
'88	NYY	45	48	.484	5th (3.5)	—
'90	CIN	91	71	.562	1st (+5)	Won WS
'91	CIN	74	88	.457	5th (20)	—
'92	CIN	90	72	.556	2nd (8)	—
'93	SEA	82	80	.506	4th (12)	—
'94	SEA	49	63	.438	3rd (2)	—
'95	SEA	79	66	.545	1st (+2)	Lost ALCS
'96	SEA	85	76	.528	2nd (4.5)	—
'97	SEA	90	72	.556	1st (+6)	Lost ALDS
'98	SEA	76	85	.472	3rd (11.5)	—
'99	SEA	79	83	.488	3rd (16)	—
'00	SEA	91	71	.562	2nd (.5)	Lost ALCS
'01	SEA	116	46	.716	1st (+14)	Lost ALCS
'02	SEA	93	69	.574	3rd (10)	—
'03	TB	63	99	.389	5th (38)	—
'04	TB	70	91	.435	4th (3.5)	—
'05	TB	67	95	.414	5th (28)	—
'07	CHC	85	77	.525	1st (+2)	Lost NLDS
Totals		**1,604**	**1,497**	**.517**	**5 div. titles**	**6 app.**

Chicago Tribune Photo by BONNIE TRAFELET

OTHER CUBS

In addition to the 25 players shown on these cards, the following players appeared in games for the Cubs in 2008:

PITCHERS (10)

☐ Jose Ascanio ☐ Rich Hill
☐ Chad Fox ☐ Jon Lieber
☐ Sean Gallagher ☐ Carmen Pignatiello
☐ Angel Guzman ☐ Randy Wells
☐ Kevin Hart ☐ Michael Wuertz

HITTERS (6)

☐ Koyie Hill ☐ Matt Murton
☐ Micah Hoffpauir ☐ Eric Patterson
☐ Casey McGehee ☐ Felix Pie

Chicago Tribune

RICH HARDEN
NO. 40 ★ PITCHER

HT: 6-1 • WT: 195 • BATS: L • THROWS: R
BORN: 11/30/81 in Victoria, B.C., Canada
HOW ACQ'D: Trade with A's (2008)

CAREER PITCHING STATS

YR.	TEAM	G	IP	H	W	L	BB	SO	ERA
'03	OAK	15	74.2	72	5	4	40	67	4.46
'04	OAK	31	189.2	171	11	7	81	167	3.99
'05	OAK	22	128.0	93	10	5	43	121	2.53
'06	OAK	9	46.2	31	4	0	26	49	4.24
'07	OAK	7	25.2	18	1	2	11	27	2.45
Totals		**84**	**464.2**	**385**	**31**	**18**	**201**	**431**	**3.60**

2008 HIGHLIGHTS

★ Made his first start of the season in Japan, pitching the A's to a 5-1 win over Boston in the Tokyo Dome on March 26.

★ Traded to the Cubs along with Chad Gaudin from the Oakland A's on July 8.

★ Team won seven straight games he started beginning July 31 in Milwaukee.

Chicago Tribune Photo by BONNIE TRAFELET

CHAD GAUDIN
NO. 57 ★ PITCHER

HT: 5-10 • WT: 190 • BATS: R • THROWS: R
BORN: 3/24/83 in New Orleans
HOW ACQ'D: Trade with A's (2008)

CAREER PITCHING STATS

YR.	TEAM	G	IP	H	W	L	SV	BB	SO	ERA
'03	TB	15	40.0	37	2	0	0	16	23	3.60
'04	TB	26	42.2	59	1	2	0	16	30	4.85
'05	TOR	5	13.0	13	1	3	0	6	12	13.15
'06	OAK	55	64.0	51	4	2	2	42	36	3.09
'07	OAK	34	199.1	205	11	13	0	100	154	4.42
Totals		**135**	**359.0**	**383**	**19**	**20**	**2**	**180**	**255**	**4.46**

2008 HIGHLIGHTS

★ Traded to the Cubs along with Rich Harden from the Oakland A's on July 8 in a six-player deal.

★ Pitched two innings of scoreless relief against the Giants on July 13.

★ Won his first game as a Cub on July 27, working a 1-2-3 seventh against the Marlins.

Chicago Tribune Photo by PHIL VELASQUEZ

RYAN DEMPSTER
NO. 46 ★ PITCHER

HT: 6-2 • WT: 215 • BATS: R • THROWS: R
BORN: 5/3/77 in Gibsons, B.C., Canada
HOW ACQ'D: Signed as free agent (2004)

CAREER PITCHING STATS

YR.	TEAM	G	IP	H	W	L	BB	SO	ERA
'98	FLA	14	54.2	72	1	5	38	35	7.08
'99	FLA	25	147.0	146	7	8	93	126	4.71
'00	FLA	33	226.1	210	14	10	97	209	3.66
'01	FLA	34	211.1	218	15	12	112	171	4.94
'02	FLA	18	120.1	126	5	8	55	87	4.79
'02	CIN	15	88.2	102	5	5	38	66	6.19
'03	CIN	22	115.2	134	3	7	70	84	6.54
'04	CHC	23	20.2	16	1	1	13	18	3.92
'05	CHC	63	92.0	83	5	3	49	89	3.13
'06	CHC	74	75.0	77	1	9	36	67	4.80
'07	CHC	66	66.2	59	2	7	30	55	4.73
Totals		**387**	**1,218.1**	**1,243**	**59**	**75**	**631**	**1,007**	**4.82**

2008 HIGHLIGHTS

★ Won his 16th game Sept. 16 while handing CC Sabathia his first NL loss.

Chicago Tribune Photo by PHIL VELASQUEZ

CARLOS MARMOL
NO. 49 ★ PITCHER

HT: 6-2 • WT: 180 • BATS: R • THROWS: R
BORN: 10/14/82 in Bonao, D.R.
HOW ACQ'D: Amateur free agent (1999)

CAREER PITCHING STATS

YR.	TEAM	G	IP	H	W	L	SV	BB	SO	ERA
'06	CHC	19	77	71	5	7	0	59	59	6.08
'07	CHC	59	69.1	41	5	1	1	35	96	1.43
		78	**146.1**	**112**	**10**	**8**	**1**	**94**	**155**	**3.87**

2008 HIGHLIGHTS

★ Recorded a 2.09 ERA over his first 37 appearances of the season.

★ Named to the NL All-Star team to replace injured teammate Kerry Wood.

★ Retired all three batters he faced in the 13th inning of the All-Star Game.

★ Broke club record for holds with his 16th.

★ Just 10th Cubs reliever since 1956 to strike out more than 100 batters.

Chicago Tribune Photo by CHARLES CHERNEY

TED LILLY
NO. 30 ★ PITCHER

HT: 6-1 • WT: 190 • BATS: L • THROWS: L
BORN: 1/4/76 in Torrance, Calif.
HOW ACQ'D: Signed as free agent (2006)

CAREER PITCHING STATS

YR.	TEAM	G	IP	H	W	L	BB	SO	ERA
'99	MON	9	23.2	30	0	1	9	28	7.61
'00	NYY	7	8.0	8	0	0	5	11	5.63
'01	NYY	26	120.2	126	5	6	51	112	5.37
'02	NYY	16	76.2	57	3	6	24	59	3.40
'02	OAK	6	23.1	23	2	1	7	18	4.63
'03	OAK	32	178.1	179	12	10	58	147	4.34
'04	TOR	32	197.1	171	12	10	89	168	4.06
'05	TOR	25	126.1	135	10	11	58	96	5.56
'06	TOR	32	181.2	179	15	13	81	160	4.31
'07	CHC	34	207.0	181	15	8	55	174	3.83
Totals		**219**	**1,143.0**	**1,089**	**74**	**66**	**437**	**973**	**4.46**

2008 HIGHLIGHTS

★ Recorded 1,000th career strikeout on May 3.

★ Threw seven innings of one-hit ball against Houston on Sept. 15.

Chicago Tribune Photo by PHIL VELASQUEZ

BOB HOWRY
NO. 62 ★ PITCHER

HT: 6-5 • WT: 220 • BATS: L • THROWS: R
BORN: 8/4/73 in Phoenix
HOW ACQ'D: Signed as free agent (2005)

CAREER PITCHING STATS

YR.	TEAM	G	IP	H	W	L	SV	BB	SO	ERA
'98	CWS	44	54.1	37	0	3	9	19	51	3.15
'99	CWS	69	67.2	58	5	3	28	38	80	3.59
'00	CWS	65	71.0	54	2	4	7	29	60	3.17
'01	CWS	69	78.2	85	4	5	5	30	64	4.69
'02	CWS	47	50.2	45	2	2	0	17	31	3.91
'02	BOS	20	18.0	22	1	3	0	4	14	5.00
'03	BOS	4	4.1	11	0	0	0	3	4	12.46
'04	CLE	37	42.2	37	4	2	0	12	39	2.74
'05	CLE	79	73.0	49	7	4	3	16	48	2.47
'06	CHC	84	76.2	70	4	5	5	17	71	3.17
'07	CHC	78	81.1	76	6	7	8	19	72	3.32
Totals		**596**	**618.1**	**544**	**35**	**38**	**65**	**204**	**534**	**3.49**

2008 HIGHLIGHTS

★ Earned wins in consecutive outings, Aug. 5 and 8.

Chicago Tribune Photo by BONNIE TRAFELET

CUBS

JASON MARQUIS
PITCHER

CUBS

SEAN MARSHALL
PITCHER

CUBS

JEFF SAMARDZIJA
PITCHER

CUBS

2008 ALL-STAR

KERRY WOOD
PITCHER

CUBS

2008 ALL-STAR

CARLOS ZAMBRANO
PITCHER

CUBS

HENRY BLANCO
CATCHER

CUBS

2008 ALL-STAR

GEOVANY SOTO
CATCHER

CUBS

RONNY CEDENO
INFIELD

CUBS

MARK DeROSA
SECOND BASE / OUTFIELD

JEFF SAMARDZIJA
NO. 29 ★ PITCHER

HT: 6-5 • WT: 220 • BATS: R • THROWS: R
BORN: 1/23/85 in Merrillville, Ind.
HOW ACQ'D: 5th round draft pick (2006)

CAREER PITCHING STATS

YR.	TEAM	G	IP	H	W	L	SV	BB	SO	ERA
(Did not play in Major Leagues prior to 2008)										

2008 HIGHLIGHTS

★ Promoted from AAA Iowa on July 25, where he had been a starter, and made his major-league debut at Wrigley Field that day against Florida.

★ Converted first major-league save with two perfect innings July 27 against Florida.

★ Earned first major-league victory with 1 1/3 shutout innings Aug. 29 against Philadelphia.

★ Streak of 15 1/3 scoreless innings was snapped Sept. 1. Held opponents to .185 average over that span.

Chicago Tribune Photo by PHIL VELASQUEZ

SEAN MARSHALL
NO. 45 ★ PITCHER

HT: 6-7 • WT: 220 • BATS: L • THROWS: L
BORN: 8/30/82 in Richmond, Va.
HOW ACQ'D: 6th round draft pick (2003)

CAREER PITCHING STATS

YR.	TEAM	G	IP	H	W	L	BB	SO	ERA
'06	CHC	24	125.2	132	6	9	59	77	5.59
'07	CHC	21	103.1	107	7	8	35	67	3.92
Totals		**45**	**229.0**	**239**	**13**	**17**	**94**	**144**	**4.83**

2008 HIGHLIGHTS

★ Earned his first major-league save on April 9 against the Pirates, pitching a scoreless 15th inning.

★ Threw two perfect innings against the Giants on July 12, striking out two and winning his second game of the year. It was his first relief appearance since May 7.

★ Had streak of 1-0, 1.46 ERA in seven home relief appearances starting July 12.

Chicago Tribune Photo by PHIL VELASQUEZ

JASON MARQUIS
NO. 21 ★ PITCHER

HT: 6-1 • WT: 210 • BATS: L • THROWS: R
BORN: 8/21/78 in Manhasset, N.Y.
HOW ACQ'D: Signed as free agent (2006)

CAREER PITCHING STATS

YR.	TEAM	G	IP	H	W	L	BB	SO	ERA
'00	ATL	15	23.1	23	1	0	12	17	5.01
'01	ATL	38	129.1	113	5	6	59	98	3.48
'02	ATL	22	114.1	127	8	9	49	84	5.04
'03	ATL	21	40.2	43	0	0	18	19	5.53
'04	STL	32	201.1	215	15	7	70	138	3.71
'05	STL	33	207.0	206	13	14	69	100	4.13
'06	STL	33	194.1	221	14	16	75	96	6.02
'07	CHC	34	191.2	190	12	9	76	109	4.60
Totals		**228**	**1,102.0**	**1,138**	**68**	**61**	**428**	**661**	**4.56**

2008 HIGHLIGHTS

★ Won four of five decisions starting Aug. 6.

★ Reached double figures in wins for fifth straight year on Sept. 6, pitching into the eighth inning at Cincinnati.

Chicago Tribune Photo by PHIL VELASQUEZ

HENRY BLANCO
NO. 24 ★ CATCHER

HT: 5-11 • WT: 220 • BATS: R • THROWS: R
BORN: 8/29/71 in Caracas, Venezuela
HOW ACQ'D: Signed as free agent (2004)

CAREER HITTING STATS

YR.	TEAM	G	AB	R	H	HR	RBI	OBP	AVG.
'97	LAD	3	5	1	2	1	1	.400	.400
'99	COL	88	263	30	61	6	28	.320	.232
'00	MIL	93	284	29	67	7	31	.318	.236
'01	MIL	104	314	33	66	6	31	.290	.210
'02	ATL	81	221	17	45	6	22	.267	.204
'03	ATL	55	151	11	30	1	13	.252	.199
'04	MIN	114	315	36	65	10	37	.260	.206
'05	CHC	54	161	16	39	6	25	.287	.242
'06	CHC	74	241	23	64	6	37	.304	.266
'07	CHC	22	54	3	9	0	4	.193	.167
Totals		**688**	**2,009**	**199**	**448**	**49**	**229**	**.287**	**.223**

2008 HIGHLIGHTS

★ Hit safely in 19 of his first 23 starts. Cubs were 14-9 in those 23 games.

Chicago Tribune Photo by PHIL VELASQUEZ

CARLOS ZAMBRANO
NO. 38 ★ PITCHER

HT: 6-5 • WT: 255 • BATS: S • THROWS: R
BORN: 6/1/81 in Puerto Cabello, Venezuela
HOW ACQ'D: Amateur free agent (1997)

CAREER PITCHING STATS

YR.	TEAM	G	IP	H	W	L	BB	SO	ERA
'01	CHC	6	7.2	11	1	2	8	4	15.26
'02	CHC	32	108.1	94	4	8	63	93	3.66
'03	CHC	32	214.0	188	13	11	94	168	3.11
'04	CHC	31	209.2	174	16	8	81	188	2.75
'05	CHC	33	223.1	170	14	6	86	202	3.26
'06	CHC	33	214.0	162	16	7	115	210	3.41
'07	CHC	34	216.1	187	18	13	101	177	3.95
Totals		**201**	**1,193.1**	**986**	**82**	**55**	**548**	**1,042**	**3.41**

2008 HIGHLIGHTS

★ Set Cubs career mark for home runs by a pitcher with his 14th on July 19.

★ Named to third NL All-Star team (2004, '06).

★ Tossed first no-hitter for Cubs in 36 years Sept. 14 against Houston.

Chicago Tribune Photo by PHIL VELASQUEZ

KERRY WOOD
NO. 34 ★ PITCHER

HT: 6-5 • WT: 210 • BATS: R • THROWS: R
BORN: 6/16/77 in Irving, Texas
HOW ACQ'D: 1st round pick (1995)

CAREER PITCHING STATS

YR.	TEAM	G	IP	H	W	L	BB	SO	ERA
'98	CHC	26	166.2	117	13	6	85	233	3.40
'00	CHC	23	137.0	112	8	7	87	132	4.80
'01	CHC	28	174.1	127	12	6	92	217	3.36
'02	CHC	33	213.2	169	12	11	97	217	3.66
'03	CHC	32	211.0	152	14	11	100	266	3.20
'04	CHC	22	140.1	127	8	9	51	144	3.72
'05	CHC	21	66.0	52	3	4	26	77	4.23
'06	CHC	4	19.2	19	1	2	8	13	4.12
'07	CHC	22	24.1	18	1	1	13	24	3.33
Totals		**211**	**1,153.0**	**893**	**72**	**57**	**559**	**1,323**	**3.67**

2008 HIGHLIGHTS

★ Converted 16 straight saves at Wrigley Field.

★ Named to the NL All-Star team, but was unable to participate because of injury.

Chicago Tribune Photo by PHIL VELASQUEZ

MARK DeROSA
NO. 7 ★ 2B / OF

HT: 6-1 • WT: 205 • BATS: R • THROWS: R
BORN: 2/26/75 in Passaic, N.J.
HOW ACQ'D: Signed as free agent (2006)

CAREER HITTING STATS

YR.	TEAM	G	AB	R	H	HR	RBI	OBP	AVG.
'98	ATL	5	3	2	1	0	0	.333	.333
'99	ATL	7	8	0	0	0	0	.000	.000
'00	ATL	22	13	9	4	0	3	.400	.308
'01	ATL	66	161	27	47	3	20	.350	.287
'02	ATL	72	212	42	63	5	23	.339	.297
'03	ATL	103	266	40	70	6	22	.316	.263
'04	ATL	118	309	33	74	3	31	.293	.239
'05	TEX	66	148	26	36	8	20	.325	.243
'06	TEX	136	520	78	154	13	74	.357	.296
'07	CHC	149	502	64	149	10	72	.371	.293
Totals		**744**	**2,145**	**303**	**596**	**48**	**265**	**.341**	**.278**

2008 HIGHLIGHTS

★ Reached career highs with 20 homers and 83 RBIs on Sept. 6 at Cincinnati.

★ Appeared at six positions during the season.

Chicago Tribune Photo by PHIL VELASQUEZ

RONNY CEDENO
NO. 5 ★ INFIELD

HT: 6-0 • WT: 180 • BATS: R • THROWS: R
BORN: 2/2/83 in Carabobo, Venezuela
HOW ACQ'D: Signed as free agent (1999)

CAREER HITTING STATS

YR.	TEAM	G	AB	R	H	HR	RBI	OBP	AVG.
'05	CHC	41	80	13	24	1	6	.356	.300
'06	CHC	151	534	51	131	6	41	.271	.245
'07	CHC	38	74	6	15	4	13	.231	.203
Totals		**230**	**688**	**70**	**170**	**11**	**60**	**.277**	**.247**

2008 HIGHLIGHTS

★ Batted .329 (23-for-70) in 28 games from April 19 to May 19.

★ Made his first career appearance in center field as a pinch-hitter/defensive replacement in Toronto on June 13.

★ Beginning July 24, hit .302 over a 32-game span.

Chicago Tribune Photo by PHIL VELASQUEZ

GEOVANY SOTO
NO. 18 ★ CATCHER

HT: 6-1 • WT: 225 • BATS: R • THROWS: R
BORN: 1/20/83 in San Juan, Puerto Rico
HOW ACQ'D: 11th round draft pick (2001)

CAREER HITTING STATS

YR.	TEAM	G	AB	R	H	HR	RBI	OBP	AVG.
'05	CHC	1	1	0	0	0	0	.000	.000
'06	CHC	11	25	1	5	0	2	.231	.200
'07	CHC	18	54	12	21	3	8	.433	.389
Totals		**30**	**80**	**13**	**26**	**3**	**10**	**.368**	**.325**

2008 HIGHLIGHTS

★ Was the starting catcher for the N.L. squad in the All-Star Game, the first rookie National League catcher ever to start the midsummer classic and the first Cubs catcher to start since Gabby Hartnett in 1937.

★ Earned NL Rookie of the Month honors in August for hitting .355 with 21 RBIs.

★ Broke club record for rookie homers by catcher with 20th on Aug. 26.

Chicago Tribune Photo by BONNIE TRAFELET

CUBS

MIKE FONTENOT
INFIELD

CUBS

DERREK LEE
FIRST BASE

CUBS
2008 ALL-STAR

ARAMIS RAMIREZ
THIRD BASE

CUBS

RYAN THERIOT
SHORTSTOP

CUBS

DARYLE WARD
FIRST BASE / OUTFIELD

CUBS

JIM EDMONDS
OUTFIELD

CUBS
2008 ALL-STAR

KOSUKE FUKUDOME
OUTFIELD

CUBS

REED JOHNSON
OUTFIELD

CUBS
2008 ALL-STAR

ALFONSO SORIANO
OUTFIELD

ARAMIS RAMIREZ
NO. 16 ★ THIRD BASE

HT: 6-1 • WT: 215 • BATS: R • THROWS: R
BORN: 6/25/78 in Santo Domingo, D.R.
HOW ACQ'D: Trade with Pirates (2003)

CAREER HITTING STATS

YR.	TEAM	G	AB	R	H	HR	RBI	OBP	AVG.
'98	PIT	72	251	23	59	6	24	.296	.235
'99	PIT	18	56	2	10	0	7	.254	.179
'00	PIT	73	254	19	65	6	35	.293	.256
'01	PIT	158	603	83	181	34	112	.350	.300
'02	PIT	142	522	51	122	18	71	.294	.234
'03	PIT	96	375	44	105	12	67	.330	.280
'03	CHC	63	232	31	60	15	39	.314	.259
'04	CHC	145	547	99	174	36	103	.373	.318
'05	CHC	123	463	72	140	31	92	.358	.302
'06	CHC	157	594	93	173	38	119	.352	.291
'07	CHC	132	506	72	157	26	101	.366	.310
Totals		**1,179**	**4,403**	**589**	**1,246**	**222**	**770**	**.336**	**.283**

2008 HIGHLIGHTS
★ Went 6-for-13 with four homers and eight RBI in the June 20-22 series against the Sox.

Chicago Tribune — Photo by PHIL VELASQUEZ

DERREK LEE
NO. 25 ★ FIRST BASE

HT: 6-5 • WT: 245 • BATS: R • THROWS: R
BORN: 9/6/75 in Sacramento
HOW ACQ'D: Trade with Marlins (2003)

CAREER HITTING STATS

YR.	TEAM	G	AB	R	H	HR	RBI	OBP	AVG.
'97	SD	22	54	9	14	1	4	.365	.259
'98	FLA	141	454	62	106	17	74	.318	.233
'99	FLA	70	218	21	45	5	20	.263	.206
'00	FLA	158	477	70	134	28	70	.368	.281
'01	FLA	158	561	83	158	21	75	.346	.282
'02	FLA	162	581	95	157	27	86	.378	.270
'03	FLA	155	539	91	146	31	92	.379	.271
'04	CHC	161	605	90	168	32	98	.356	.278
'05	CHC	158	594	120	199	46	107	.418	.335
'06	CHC	50	175	30	50	8	30	.368	.286
'07	CHC	150	567	91	180	22	82	.400	.317
Totals		**1,385**	**4,825**	**762**	**1,357**	**238**	**738**	**.367**	**.281**

2008 HIGHLIGHTS
★ Matched career high in hits, going 5-for-5 with 3 RBI against the White Sox on June 28.

Chicago Tribune — Photo by PHIL VELASQUEZ

MIKE FONTENOT
NO. 17 ★ INFIELD

HT: 5-8 • WT: 170 • BATS: L • THROWS: R
BORN: 6/9/80 in Slidell, La.
HOW ACQ'D: Trade with Orioles (2005)

CAREER HITTING STATS

YR.	TEAM	G	AB	R	H	HR	RBI	OBP	AVG.
'05	CHC	7	2	4	0	0	0	.600	.000
'07	CHC	86	234	32	65	3	29	.336	.278
Totals		**93**	**236**	**36**	**65**	**3**	**29**	**.341**	**.275**

2008 HIGHLIGHTS
★ Homered and doubled with two RBI in consecutive games, July 8 and 10.
★ Went 3-for-4 with a double, homer, three runs and three RBI in Houston on June 20.
★ Homered June 21 vs. the White Sox, contributing to the Cubs' nine-run fourth inning.
★ Had a pinch-hit three-run double, providing the winning margin against Florida on July 27.

Chicago Tribune — Photo by PHIL VELASQUEZ

JIM EDMONDS
NO. 15 ★ OUTFIELD

HT: 6-1 • WT: 210 • BATS: L • THROWS: L
BORN: 6/27/70 in Fullerton, Calif.
HOW ACQ'D: Signed as free agent (2008)

CAREER HITTING STATS

YR.	TEAM	G	AB	R	H	HR	RBI	OBP	AVG.
'93	CAL	18	61	5	15	0	4	.270	.246
'94	CAL	94	289	35	79	5	37	.343	.273
'95	CAL	141	558	120	162	33	107	.352	.290
'96	CAL	114	431	73	131	27	66	.375	.304
'97	ANA	133	502	82	146	26	80	.368	.291
'98	ANA	154	599	115	184	25	91	.368	.307
'99	ANA	55	204	34	51	5	23	.339	.250
'00	STL	152	525	129	155	42	108	.411	.295
'01	STL	150	500	95	152	30	110	.410	.304
'02	STL	144	476	96	148	28	83	.420	.311
'03	STL	137	447	89	123	39	89	.385	.275
'04	STL	153	498	102	150	42	111	.418	.301
'05	STL	142	467	88	123	29	89	.385	.263
'06	STL	110	350	52	90	19	70	.350	.257
'07	STL	117	365	39	92	12	53	.325	.252
Totals		**1,814**	**6,272**	**1,154**	**1,801**	**362**	**1,121**	**.379**	**.287**

2008 HIGHLIGHTS
★ Two homers in fourth inning vs. Sox, 6/21.

Chicago Tribune — Photo by PHIL VELASQUEZ

DARYLE WARD
NO. 33 ★ 1B / OF

HT: 6-2 • WT: 240 • BATS: L • THROWS: L
BORN: 6/27/75 in Lynwood, Calif.
HOW ACQ'D: Signed as free agent (2006)

CAREER HITTING STATS

YR.	TEAM	G	AB	R	H	HR	RBI	OBP	AVG.
'98	HOU	4	3	1	1	0	1	.500	.333
'99	HOU	64	150	11	41	8	30	.311	.273
'00	HOU	119	264	36	68	20	47	.295	.258
'01	HOU	95	213	21	56	9	39	.323	.263
'02	HOU	136	453	41	125	12	72	.324	.276
'03	LAD	52	109	6	20	0	9	.211	.183
'04	PIT	79	293	39	73	15	57	.305	.249
'05	PIT	133	407	46	106	12	63	.318	.260
'06	ATL	20	26	2	8	1	7	.333	.308
'06	WAS	78	104	15	32	6	19	.390	.308
'07	CHC	79	110	16	36	3	19	.436	.327
Totals		**859**	**2,132**	**234**	**566**	**86**	**362**	**.321**	**.265**

2008 HIGHLIGHTS
★ Was the DH June 27 and started in right field June 28 against the White Sox, going 4-for-9 in the two games.

Chicago Tribune — Photo by JOSÉ M. OSORIO

RYAN THERIOT
NO. 2 ★ SHORTSTOP

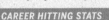

HT: 5-11 • WT: 175 • BATS: R • THROWS: R
BORN: 12/7/79 in Baton Rouge, La.
HOW ACQ'D: 3rd round draft pick (2001)

CAREER HITTING STATS

YR.	TEAM	G	AB	R	H	HR	RBI	OBP	AVG.
'05	CHC	9	13	3	2	0	0	.214	.154
'06	CHC	53	134	34	44	3	16	.412	.328
'07	CHC	148	537	80	143	3	45	.326	.266
Totals		**210**	**684**	**117**	**189**	**6**	**61**	**.341**	**.276**

2008 HIGHLIGHTS
★ Had a career-high 13-game hitting streak snapped against Arizona on July 21. Hit .439 (25-for-57) during the streak.
★ Went 3-for-5 against St. Louis on July 6.
★ Reached base safely in 17 straight games from July 2-23.
★ Hit over .300 in April, May, June and July before falling to .281 for August.

Chicago Tribune — Photo by PHIL VELASQUEZ

ALFONSO SORIANO
NO. 12 ★ OUTFIELD

HT: 6-1 • WT: 180 • BATS: R • THROWS: R
BORN: 1/7/76 in San Pedro de Macoris, D.R.
HOW ACQ'D: Signed as free agent (2006)

CAREER HITTING STATS

YR.	TEAM	G	AB	R	H	HR	RBI	OBP	AVG.
'99	NYY	9	8	2	1	1	1	.125	.125
'00	NYY	22	50	5	9	2	3	.196	.180
'01	NYY	158	574	77	154	18	73	.304	.268
'02	NYY	156	696	128	209	39	102	.332	.300
'03	NYY	156	682	114	198	38	91	.338	.290
'04	TEX	145	608	77	170	28	91	.324	.280
'05	TEX	156	637	102	171	36	104	.309	.268
'06	WAS	159	647	119	179	46	95	.351	.277
'07	CHC	135	579	97	173	33	70	.337	.299
Totals		**1,096**	**4,481**	**721**	**1,264**	**241**	**630**	**.327**	**.282**

2008 HIGHLIGHTS
★ Named N.L. Player of the Week (ending May 18), hitting .516 with seven home runs.
★ Elected by the fans to start the All-Star Game but could not appear due to injury.

Chicago Tribune — Photo by PHIL VELASQUEZ

REED JOHNSON
NO. 9 ★ OUTFIELD

HT: 5-10 • WT: 180 • BATS: R • THROWS: R
BORN: 12/8/76 in Riverside, Calif.
HOW ACQ'D: Signed as free agent (2008)

CAREER HITTING STATS

YR.	TEAM	G	AB	R	H	HR	RBI	OBP	AVG.
'03	TOR	114	412	79	121	10	52	.353	.294
'04	TOR	141	537	68	145	10	61	.320	.270
'05	TOR	142	398	55	107	8	58	.332	.269
'06	TOR	134	461	86	158	12	49	.390	.319
'07	TOR	79	375	21	66	2	14	.305	.236
Totals		**610**	**2,083**	**319**	**585**	**42**	**234**	**.342**	**.281**

2008 HIGHLIGHTS
★ Went 3-for-4 with two runs, a double, his second career grand slam and 4 RBI against Florida on July 25.
★ In 40 games after July 12, hit .357, including a five-game hitting streak Aug. 13-17.
★ Was hit by pitch to bring in the winning run in the 11th inning against Atlanta on June 12.

Chicago Tribune — Photo by PHIL VELASQUEZ

KOSUKE FUKUDOME
NO. 1 ★ OUTFIELD

HT: 6-0 • WT: 187 • BATS: L • THROWS: R
BORN: 4/26/77 in Osaki, Japan
HOW ACQ'D: Signed as free agent (2007)

CAREER HITTING STATS

YR.	TEAM	G	AB	R	H	HR	RBI	OBP	AVG.
(Did not play in Major Leagues prior to 2008)									

2008 HIGHLIGHTS
★ In his first game as a Cub, went 3-for-3 with a walk and a ninth-inning, game-tying home run against Milwaukee on March 31.
★ Hit a solo home run in the first inning that accounted for the game-winning RBI against St. Louis on July 4.
★ Was elected by the fans to start in center field for the National League in the All-Star Game.
★ Hit first major-league pinch homer Aug. 24 vs. Nationals.

Chicago Tribune — Photo by NUCCIO DiNUZZO

CUBS SEASONS, 1903-2007

Although the franchise dates from 1876, they did not become the Cubs until 1903.

SEASON	WON	LOST	PLACE	PCT.	GB
1903	82	56	3	.594	8
1904	93	60	2	.608	13
1905	92	61	3	.601	13
1906			1	.763	
Lost World Series to the White Sox, 4 games to 2				
1907			1	.704	
Won World Series over the Tigers, 4 games to 0				
1908			1	.643	
Won World Series over the Tigers, 4 games to 1				
1909	104	49	2	.680	6.5
1910			1	.675	
Lost World Series to the Philadelphia A's, 4 games to 2				
1911	92	62	2	.597	7.5
1912	91	59	3	.607	11.5
1913	88	65	3	.575	13.5
1914	78	76	4	.506	16.5
1915	73	80	4	.477	17.5
1916	67	86	5	.438	26.5
1917	74	80	5	.481	24
1918			1	.651	
Lost World Series to the Red Sox, 4 games to 1				
1919	75	65	3	.536	21
1920	75	79	5	.487	18
1921	64	89	7	.418	30
1922	80	74	5	.519	13
1923	83	71	4	.539	12.5
1924	81	72	5	.529	12
1925	68	86	8	.442	27.5
1926	82	72	4	.532	7
1927	85	68	4	.556	8.5
1928	91	63	3	.591	4
1929			1	.645	
Lost World Series to the Philadelphia A's, 4 games to 1				
1930	90	64	2	.584	2
1931	84	70	3	.545	17
1932			1	.584	
Lost World Series to the Yankees, 4 games to 0				
1933	86	68	3	.558	6
1934	86	65	3	.570	8
1935			1	.649	
Lost World Series to the Tigers, 4 games to 2				
1936	87	67	2	.565	5
1937	93	61	2	.604	3
1938			1	.586	
Lost World Series to the Yankees, 4 games to 0				
1939	84	70	4	.545	13
1940	75	79	5	.487	25.5
1941	70	84	6	.455	30
1942	68	86	6	.442	38
1943	74	79	5	.484	30.5
1944	75	79	4	.487	30
1945			1	.636	
Lost World Series to the Tigers, 4 games to 3				
1946	82	71	3	.536	14.5
1947	69	85	6	.448	25
1948	64	90	8	.416	27.5
1949	61	93	8	.396	36
1950	64	89	7	.418	26.5
1951	62	92	8	.403	34.5
1952	77	77	5	.500	19.5
1953	65	89	7	.422	40
1954	64	90	7	.416	33
1955	72	81	6	.471	26
1956	60	94	8	.390	33
1957	62	92	7	.403	33
1958	72	82	5	.468	20
1959	74	80	5	.481	13
1960	60	94	7	.390	35
1961	64	90	7	.416	29
1962	59	103	9	.364	42.5
1963	82	80	7	.506	17
1964	76	86	8	.469	17
1965	72	90	8	.444	25
1966	59	103	10	.364	36
1967	87	74	3	.540	14
1968	84	78	3	.519	13
1969	92	70	2	.568	8
1970	84	78	2	.519	5
1971	83	79	3	.512	14
1972	85	70	2	.548	11
1973	77	84	5	.478	5
1974	66	96	6	.407	22
1975	75	87	5	.463	17.5
1976	75	87	4	.463	26
1977	81	81	4	.500	20
1978	79	83	3	.488	11
1979	80	82	5	.494	18
1980	64	98	6	.395	27
1981	38	65	6	.369	21.5
1982	73	89	5	.451	19
1983	71	91	5	.438	19
1984			1	.596	
Lost NLCS to the Padres, 3 games to 2				
1985	77	84	4	.478	23.5
1986	70	90	5	.438	37
1987	76	85	6	.472	18.5
1988	77	85	4	.475	24
1989			1	.574	
Lost NLCS to the Giants, 4 games to 1				
1990	77	85	4	.475	18
1991	77	83	4	.481	20
1992	78	84	4	.481	18
1993	84	78	4	.519	13
1994	49	64	5	.434	16.5
1995	73	71	3	.507	12
1996	76	86	4	.469	12
1997	68	94	5	.420	16
1998			2	.552	
Lost NLDS to the Braves, 3 games to 0				
1999	67	95	6	.414	30
2000	65	97	6	.401	30
2001	88	74	3	.543	5
2002	67	95	5	.414	30
2003			1	.543	
Beat Braves in NLDS, 3-2; lost NLCS to Marlins, 4-3				
2004	89	73	3	.549	16
2005	79	83	4	.488	21
2006	66	96	6	.407	17.5
2007			1	.525	
Lost NLDS to the Diamondbacks, 3 games to 0				
2008					

CREDITS

PHIL VELASQUEZ

CHICAGO TRIBUNE

EDITOR Gerould W. Kern
MANAGING EDITOR Jane Hirt
EDITORIAL PAGE EDITOR R. Bruce Dold
EDITOR/DIGITAL MEDIA Bill Adee
ASSOCIATE EDITOR Joycelyn Winnecke

This Is the Year!
The Historic 2008 Chicago Cubs

SPORTS EDITORS Dan McGrath and Mike Kellams
ART DIRECTOR Joan Cairney
GRAPHICS EDITOR Stephen Layton
PHOTO EDITORS Robin Daughtridge and Todd Panagopoulos
COPY EDITOR Tom Carkeek
IMAGING TECHNICIAN Christine Bruno
PROJECT MANAGERS Chuck Burke and Susan Zukrow